Freakishly Effective
Leadership
for Network Marketing

RAY HIGDON • THE HIGDON GROUP

Published by

SHORT BOOKS. BIG IDEAS.

Success in 100 Pages
www.SuccessIn100Pages.com

ISBN 978-1-947814-96-7

Copyright © March 2019

All rights reserved.

I Want to <u>Personally</u> Show You How It's Possible to Create a Remarkable Brand While Still Building Duplication in Your Team

Learn How To:

- ⊘ Attract people to you by designing a powerful brand

- ⊘ Generate more leads of people that want to join your opportunity or buy your product or service

- ⊘ Increase your duplication faster than ever before (especially when you just get someone started)

- ⊘ Simplify your branding strategy and maximize your results in a fraction of the time

- ⊘ Create curiosity posts for social media and the #1 secret to effective social media engagement and results (examples included)

- ⊘ Effectively tell your story on social media and get others to duplicate (it is way simpler than you think)

- ⊘ And much more!

IF YOU'RE TIRED OF USING BRANDING STRATEGIES THAT JUST DON'T DUPLICATE, GET YOUR PLAYBOOK AT:

www.brandingduplicationplaybook.com

FOREWORD BY
LARRY & TAYLOR THOMPSON

When we were looking to build our brand online, we were referred to Ray and Jessica Higdon by several of our clients.

We met Ray in early 2011, while consulting for a Network Marketing company where Ray was the number-one earner. We'd seen him on a lot of social media platforms and felt very confident that he could help us with our business branding.

We knew we had the right guy after we found some videos of Ray going over his notes from one of the trainings we'd conducted. It was amazing to see how he'd metabolized the content with a unique ability to not just communicate the highlights, but also the important nuances, to his audience.

We are so grateful we engaged Ray in helping us build *our* brand. His knowledge about marketing, coupled with his understanding about networking, make him a rare breed.

We have worked with a lot of companies, from owners to top leaders, and can say that Ray totally embodies what we consider to be a great leader. Most people associate "leaders" by the amount of money you make, your rank, or the title you hold within the company's pay plan. Ray understands what we've always taught: that leadership is not about rank, or how much money has been earned, but about doing the daily activities that enable growth.

Ray knows what it truly means to be a leader—always leading by example. He knows that a person cannot be called a leader if no one is following. Through his work ethic, his heart to serve and give back—and certainly by the way he treats people—Ray has created a tribe of followers who adore him.

Of all the students over the last 50 years that we've had the privilege of working with, Ray has one of the sharpest, clearest minds that we've ever experienced. Ray has a great talent as a coach, mentor, and teacher. He understands one of our core philosophies, which is: *"Never let what you have to say be so important that you miss what your students need to hear."*

Trust us when we tell you—this book contains what you need to hear. Many times we've shared information in the morning, and by the end of the day, Ray had already metabolized the philosophical, strategic thinking behind the training and implemented it for his students.

Ray has the unique characteristic of having a personality that blends and works well with so many people. He communicates with empathy, strength, passion, and encouragement—regardless of the age or experience of the person he's working with. Such a rare trait!

We feel very honored to have been asked to be a part of this book. And we're grateful not just for the business relationship we have with Ray, but, more importantly, the personal relationship that has been built between us. We just hope that as you read this book you can take what's being said, digest it, metabolize it, and go out and implement it.

-Larry & Taylor Thompson

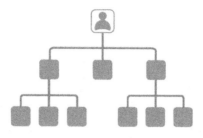

Introduction:

Thank you for making the decision to invest in this book.

In case you don't know me or my story, let me give you the quick summary: I found network marketing through a real estate partner of mine. After looking at the business model and really studying it, I knew it was a good option for me, but I didn't know what I was doing and did just about everything wrong. I went through 11 companies over a three-year period and never had a major success. During that same time, the real estate market crashed, and I ended up losing everything. I was in personal foreclosure, being chased by bill collectors and was over 1 million dollars in debt.

On July 15, 2009, I had a new vision. Sick and tired of being a victim, I got truly serious about network marketing. I worked relentlessly and prospected like crazy. I quickly became the number-one earner in that company. My girlfriend (now wife) Jessica had become extremely successful using social media to build her business and became the top female earner.

When we started really crushing it using social media, way before hardly anyone else was, we started getting asked to teach teams and leaders how to do it too. Without intending to have a coaching and training business, we had one. And we found that we loved it and felt that we could help the profession better if we focused on helping companies and leaders. We retired in early 2016 from actively building and although we miss all the team activities, we have been able to make a bigger impact which is our purpose.

In its first year, our private group, Rank Makers, helped create over 3,500 rank advancements in companies all over the world. Rank Makers is how we help leaders the most by helping get their people into action.

The Purpose of This Book

So, what exactly is the purpose of this book? In a nutshell, it's to:

- *Simplify what leadership in network marketing is truly about.*

- *Lay out what leaders should (and should not) be doing with their time.*

- *Give concrete advice on common mistakes that can sabotage your growth.*

- *Help you create a team where every level of performer is happy, excited and never wants to leave!*

And perhaps—more than anything else—this book will give you what you need to know and do to deliver financial results over time, for yourself and other members of your team.

You may not believe this, but I wish we operated in a world where there was no demand for this book. Seriously. I wish all leaders already knew how to lead effectively—because, even though it would reduce some of the need for what my company teaches—it would mean that more leaders were already functional, and their teams were already achieving peak levels of performance. But there is a need.

A serious need.

How This Book Is Organized

As you read, you'll see the topics jump around a bit. This is not an accident—it has been done *intentionally*, by design. The reason is, when people *think* they already know what their strengths and weaknesses are, they'll go straight to the sections they perceive as needs and ignore the rest.

We don't want you to approach this book that way. We want you to read the whole damn thing. You never know which section of a book—which paragraph, or single sentence—can make the whole book worthwhile and have a major impact on your life.

For the same reason, the topics in this book are not presented in order of order of importance, *because they are all important.*

What's more, some things in this book might even seem like they don't belong—that they don't fall under the topic umbrella of "leadership."

Trust me: *Every topic included on the following pages has an impact on your long-term ability to become a freakishly effective leader.* So, be patient—the pieces of the leadership-puzzle will all connect by the time we're finished.

The truth is, many people say they want to be great leaders, but they're unwilling to learn the skills and/or unwilling to do the things that are necessary to succeed.

The good news is, there are little things you can do—starting today, from wherever you are—that will set you on the right path.

So, the question is: *Are you truly interested in becoming a success in network marketing by becoming a freakishly effective leader?*

If the answer is yes, I'll meet you on the next page...

Good, you're here.

Let's start with a basic question...

What Is the Definition of a Great Leader?

This is a good place to start, since it may not be what you think.

I say this because some people have a skewed view of what network marketing leadership looks like. They see the leader who must be working a million hours a week. They see someone who is hardcore in the face of their team pushing everyone to make more sales, and constantly on the phone, answering questions and managing their team like the manager of a sales team.

If that sounds like you and you are getting burnt out, this book will free you from those shackles AND will help you realize that your behavior, although well-intentioned, has been sabotaging your income and the growth of your team.

Shocked already?

You should be.

From coaching leaders with teams of 10,000 all the way up to those with teams of 700,000, we have found that most leaders do NOT have a healthy perspective on how a network marketing leader should operate. It's so much easier than the majority of leaders make it.

So, What IS the Role of a Leader?

One of the many coaching firms we have hired over the years is a company called Gazelle's. They specialize in scaling companies and although this kind of company is simply not needed for an individual network marketing leader as network marketing has built in scaling principles, it was very helpful for our coaching and training company.

The owner of Gazelle's is a man named Verne Harnish. Verne gave the most beautiful and simple explanation for the role of a leader.

Now, if you ask other leaders what the role of a leader is (and we have), they will say that the role of a leader is to inspire others, to be the example or something similar. While those are great ideas, we prefer what Verne says which is perfectly applicable to network marketing.

Verne says the role of the leader is simply,

"To make it easy."

You may be wondering, to make WHAT easy?!

In the content of this book, we will be showing you how to make it easy for your teammates to see themselves as leaders and how they can rank advance all while NOT consuming every minute of your day.

You see, when you are a workaholic leader performing as a sales manager you do two bad things:

ONE... you turn off anyone not making sales and make them feel like they are disappointing you and the team.

TWO... you show up in a way that others don't want to show up, so they sabotage themselves from ever getting to your rank.

Again, we are going to show you, how to make it E-A-S-Y.

··

Wisdom From Top Network Marketing Leader & TEC Member

RYAN HIGGINS:

Great leaders in our profession are coaches with a passion for developing and helping people become successful, by inspiring their people through a shared vision. They create an environment where people feel valued and fulfilled.

The most common mistake I see leaders make is when they tell their team what to do. They need to *lead by example* and show them the way.

To be a great leader, you need to stay plugged in with your other leaders to know when they need help or guidance. Many of them will not ask for help or guidance.

Some leaders struggle when it comes to dealing with the pressure of having everyone come to them, looking for the right answer to their questions. For some, that is overwhelming.

Another struggle is when a leader tries to be so perfect. This can actually backfire because you're not attractive anymore to your prospects, like you were in the beginning, when you were relatable.

Being a network marketing leader lets you impact so many people in so many ways, being a good resource for someone to come to. And, for me, the feeling of being fulfilled—knowing you have helped someone become a better person, not just in their business but in their life—is awesome.

··

The Best Leaders Are Masters of the Basics

In network marketing, the basics include learning and sharing stories, using the system, basic human communications, understanding and developing the team culture (more on this later), and growing the community.

If you want to build the largest team you possibly can but you don't understand those basics, you are going to come up against limitations in your approach that will hold you back from getting to where you want to go.

We like to point out that a million dollars a year is a GREAT salary but tiny for a business. Stop comparing your income in network marketing to a salary and instead start seeing yourself as a business owner, which you are.

What if Your Upline Sucks?

First, it may not be that your upline sucks. It's much more likely that they have good intentions, but the way they attempt to show those intentions rubs you the wrong way or how they show up isn't meeting your expectations.

In fact, I know many million-dollar earners who didn't have the best (or any) upline. A great upline or a bad upline will still have people that produce and don't produce. Be grateful for whoever introduced you to your company as they paved the way for you to change your life but don't hinge your success on the actions or inactions of your upline.

Stop requiring your upline to be perfect for YOU to get into action.

Understand that how your upline shows up does not have to dictate how you show up.

Best Leadership Practices and What to Avoid

Here are some best practices as a leader as well as what to avoid doing:

• Do strive to make it easy. Point out the system you and your company use and how anyone can follow the system without being credible, special, an expert or have a large following.

• Don't make it all about you. I know leaders who leverage the efforts of their team to get more engagement on their personal social media profiles. I've also seen leaders message teammates telling them what the leader needs to reach the next rank begging them to help THE LEADER out. That is ridiculous. The team is not there to help YOU but the other way around.

• Do what you wish your team was doing. Don't climb up into the trainer or manager chair and bark orders at them, instead, YOU go do the work which is asking humans if they are open to your product, service or opportunity. If you believe in your company and how it helps people, why would you ever stop introducing people to it?

• Don't rule your team with an iron fist. I know uplines who think they are the boss and everyone in the team works for them. If people don't do exactly what the leader says, then the team members are chastised, passive-aggressively or even directly criticized in front of others. 100% of your team will just not be exactly the way you wish they were and that is okay. Many leaders are more focused on controlling their team than helping them get results if it means by any other way than what they suggest. I had teams of several thousand people who were NOT brought in the exact way I taught. I got compensated off them anyway and that was okay.

• Do point out what you have overcome in your life but avoid bragging or focusing on all your amazing accomplishments or what makes you special or credible. All you do when you shine a light on your credibility and specialness is make others in the team justify why you can do it, but they cannot. The best response to the leader telling their story is, "Wow, if he/she can do it, I definitely think I can too!"

The Thompson Rule

I often get asked, *"How do I get my people producing more? How do I get them making more money?"* This is a bad question. Why? Because it assumes that just because people have joined your team, they want to be top earners. They might not.

Two of our good friends—early mentors and graduates of our Top Earner Club mastermind program—are Larry and Taylor Thompson (they also wrote the foreword to this book.) More than any other trainer on the planet, Larry is someone we credit with a lot of our concepts when it comes to leadership and building an effective performance culture.

One of the things we've learned from Larry is something we call The Thompson Rule, which says:

80 percent of people who join a network marketing organization only have a desire to earn $0 to $500 a month.

Why is this important? Because (generally speaking) people who are looking to earn less than $500 a month usually have little desire to lead a team. The people in this group are not in it to inspire others and get a team of people fired up and excited. So burdening them with having to learn leadership skills is just not necessary. It would be like wanting to be a personal trainer and being told you have to learn brain surgery (not that leadership is brain surgery, but you get the point).

- *Some people are going to be your customers...*

- *Some people are going to attend events...*

- *Some people just want to sell a few products, make a few bucks here and there...*

That's it. That's all they want. There's just no reason to push *your* desires on people with just little level of desire. No one wants to be forced to learn anything over and above what they need to learn to achieve their desires—*their desires, not their leader's desires.*

The Next 15 Percent...

Now, there's a second group, around 15 percent of people on any given team who have a level of desire to earn say, $2,000 to $3,000 a month. At this level they're going to need to learn how to build and lead at least a small team. As such, developing these people to be leaders becomes somewhat important.

...And the Elite Percent

And then there are the 5 percent of people in any organization who have a true, burning desire to earn an above-average living of $25,000 a month or more. They are there to build a business and career in the profession. They truly want to achieve financial freedom. They're the drivers who are so relentlessly focused on results, you could hand them a bad set of instructions and they're still going to make it happen.

Keep in mind, however, the Thompson Rule applies to the level of desire, not the level of results. You could have people hungry to make it happen who just aren't there yet or super high results people who don't have the desire to keep growing.

The Challenge for Elite Performers

The challenge for the 5 percenters—*the drivers*—is they think everyone should be drivers just like them. This creates a massive issue in network marketing leadership, and that problem is these elite performers want to change the laws of the universe. They want to make everyone like them. The reality is, *everyone isn't like them.*

Some people have zero desire in becoming top producers. They're happy just to belong. They just want to be a part of the group. They want to take selfies with you and get a high five for simply attending the event. That's it. And there's nothing wrong with that.

I repeat: *There's nothing wrong with that.*

"Eighty percent of people who join a network marketing organization only have a desire to only earn $0 to $500 a month."

- *The Thompson Rule*

#FEL

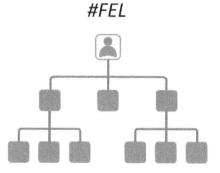

(Take a picture of this page and use #FEL)

Leading All Performers

Just so we're clear, I am in no way belittling or making fun of people who don't have the inner drive to become high achievers. These people are perfectly fine just the way they are—and you need them.

If I'm poking fun at anyone here, it might be you—*yes, you*—the leader who thinks you have some special skill or magical potion that can turn people into something other than who they are. All the wishing, hoping, pushing and prodding in the world isn't going to change that.

Worse, trying to turn people into something they are not will just blow them out of the team, reduce your income and create unnecessary churn, stress, and burnout.

Over time, the profile of just about any team will include this 80 percent who fall under the Thompson Rule. And spending 80 percent of your time trying to change the 80 percent of the team who are least likely to change is not only a waste of time, it's a mild form of insanity.

Which makes the following point more than relevant: If you have people in your organization who are not leading their people, not answering questions, and not showing up to company events, but are recruiting, my advice is to send them a *thank you card* and let it go—*it* being the need to change them into something they'll never be.

I'm serious.

Stop demanding that people be leaders. You can't force or demand someone else to be a leader! Just be grateful for what that individual *does* bring to your team and move on.

Don't Let Your Personality Get in the Way

If you personally have that elite 5 percent personality, you probably find it difficult to accept the idea that some people are happy making $0. It was for me.

I have a 5 percent personality—I just do. I'm one of those people in constant pursuit of major goals. As such, I used to think that everybody did. Which was a problem.

I would get on team calls and say things like, *"Hey everyone, if you're not prospecting 20 people a day, what are you even doing in here?"*

This wasn't very smart, nor was it very effective. *It was destructive, actually.* Your personality should never dictate what goals and dreams others should have, or how driven they should be.

Keep People Around the Campfire

One of the best analogies is to think of your team as people sitting around a campfire. What's the fire? The fire is you, as a leader, and other top leaders. The fire is also your company convention. The fire is your events. The fire is personal development, too. That's the fire.

The biggest problem in network marketing leadership is that many leaders only pay attention to those in the 5 percent elite club and ignore the rest. Remember, the 80 percent with low to no desire make up 80 percent of the volume of your organization and 80 percent of your check. Although they don't require a lot of attention, they do require some love and appreciation.

In other words, just because there are many who don't have big desires doesn't mean they aren't important. If you keep people around the campfire long enough, their level of desire might grow. If you are leading by example and working with the people who are coachable, they may step a bit closer to the fire—their level of desire may increase, they may catch a spark!

Your job as a leader is to create an amazing fire: a culture, that makes people feel good regardless of their level of desire or level of results. And, for those who do want to grow a business, make sure there are tools and resources anyone can use regardless of level of influence, expertise or background.

If you've made the mistake of making people feel unwelcome at the campfire, that they're disappointing you, or that they don't belong, they'll leave. Worse still, someday things may change. The same people who were made to feel unimportant may have a change of circumstances or sudden desire to earn more. And they'll be standing around someone else's campfire—someone who didn't ignore them and make them feel like second-class citizens.

Focus on "Inclusion," Not Exclusion

A great example of creating inclusion and not making people feel unwelcome comes from what is commonly done in church.

In church, when they "pass the plate" (or basket) to collect donations from people, some people throw in $20. Others thrown in $5-10. And a few people, for whatever reason, simply pass the plate without putting anything in at all.

Regardless of how little or much someone puts in the collection plate, the church doesn't seat them according "to class" do they? They don't push the low money droppers to the cheap seats, the culture of the church is welcoming without letting people know who is more important.

However, imagine a pastor offering an evening Bible study group that day, and then—on the way out of church—he stepped in front of you and asked if you had signed up for it. Then, when he finds out you didn't, he shakes his head and asks, "That's not good. What can we do to get you serious about God?" Can you imagine that scene?

Of course you can't—*because it would never happen.*

Different People, Different Levels of Commitment

Church leaders know three things that network marketing leaders seem to forget:

1. *Not everyone is committed to the same degree as the leader...*

2. *Not everyone has the same amount of money to contribute, and...*

3. *Not everyone wants to rise to the top rank and be a leader.*

Now, imagine something like this Bible study scenario happened to you, and then the following week it happened again. And then it happened the week after that. How many weeks would it take for you to stop going and find a new church?

But this is *exactly* what network marketing leaders do all the time! *"Hey, why aren't you at a new rank yet? I see you coming to these events, but you haven't rank advanced. I see you didn't get a check this month. How many people have you prospected this week? Only one? What's wrong with you? Are you committed or not?"*

Church leaders are too smart for any of that. They want the 80 percent of the people who can't give as much, or don't have a desire to take night classes, to stick around—because things might change.

Act Like a Gym Owner

Years ago I was a member at a gym called LA Fitness. One day, I notice this guy, and he's all geared up. He's got the headband, the wristbands, and wearing every logo-item imaginable. He's so decked-out in designer gear, he's hard not to notice. It's hard not to notice he's not in very good shape, either.

I see this guy every time I go to the gym, and he's never exercising all that hard, never really breaking a sweat. He hung out, lifted a few weights, but mostly he just chatted with people. Don't get me wrong, we talked a few times, and he was a nice enough guy.

I saw this guy for four years, and it was the same story every time. He was there when I arrived, and he was there when I left, dressed in $1,000 designer exercise garb. He barely worked out, never broke a sweat, and never seemed to lose any of his extra weight.

At $29 per month.

And this is why gym owners are smarter than most network marketing leaders. Because in all that time I never saw the gym owner walk over and say, *"Hey, man. I've been watching you come in here, and I don't see you improving. Looks like you're still the same body fat percentage as when you started. Aren't you motivated? Do you think I'm running this gym just for people to hang out?"*

Again, like with the church example, it would never happen— *not with a smart gym owner, at least.* And if they did? That guy would be gone... *and his $29 would be gone with him.*

Never forget that 80 percent of your team is happy just to be there. Which doesn't mean you have to give them a bunch of your time, but you do have to give them the courtesy of your appreciation. Because when it becomes evident that they're not welcome, they'll be gone. Make them feel good, however, and they'll stay forever.

Circumstances Change

Wait a minute, Ray. Earlier you said that you can't turn the 80 percenters into 15 percenters, let alone the elite 5 percenters. Now you're saying we should keep everyone around the campfire because someday some of those people may change.

Well, which is it? Do people change, or don't they?

What I'm saying is that you can't change people—not at the deepest level of a person's core personality, but the *circumstances* in people's lives may change. No, check that—the circumstances in people's lives *will* change.

- *They* won't have changed, *but their job situation/status may have changed.*

- *They* won't have changed, *but the relationships they have with the people in their life may have changed.*

- *Their* personality won't have changed, *but the state of their health may have changed.*

Any of these changes can have a dramatic effect on a person's drive, as well as his or her desire to sell more product, prospect more people, and generate more income. *You* didn't change the person—*the individual changed on their own*—because something in their life changed.

And when things change in people's lives—and they will—you want them to be standing around *your* campfire, not someone else's.

Things May Change in Your Life, Too

We have a coaching graduate—a really great leader named Todd Burrier. Todd built a healthy six-figure-plus business. Then, one day, he decided that his kids were at an age where he wanted to spend more time with them. Overnight, Todd went from being a hard-charging, *"let's make lots of money"* 5 percenter, to an 80 percenter in terms of his drive and business activity (*i.e.*

desire). Todd *slowed his roll,* shifting his focus from the business to his family. Because things changed for Todd.

As they do for all of us.

This is why we're very much against the pressure that some companies (and some leaders) put on people to maintain a near-psychotic level of desire. No company or individual leader should put that kind of uncomfortable pressure on others. A spouse comes down with a health issue, or the person wants to travel the world or spend time with their kids, that's their business—literally—because it is their business. That's the point of being in network marketing in the first place, right? To be able to grow your business, your way, to the level you want to grow it to.

The best leaders are there to encourage and support their people in achieving the business goals their people desire, not the goals that the leader desire.

In Todd's case, he focused on his family for years, running his business on autopilot and still bringing in a six-figure per year salary because he had built the business so solidly. And when the desire to build again struck him, he got back to work, joined our Mastermind program, and we helped him go out there and start crushing it again.

"Never forget that 80 percent of your team is happy just to be there. Make them feel good, and they'll stay forever."

-Ray Higdon

#FEL

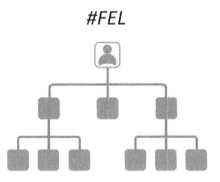

(Take a picture of this page and use #FEL)

Case Study: The Mission of the Boys & Girls Club

The Boys & Girls Club of America has a mission, and it's simple: *to get and keep kids off the streets*. They know that if they can do this, kids won't fall into any of a variety of negative behaviors, including doing and selling drugs.

The Boys & Girls Club in my area has a basketball court and all kinds of stuff to do in the clubhouse, like cooking, art, music and computers. The question is, is their mission to only get kids who want to be professional athletes off the street? Or just musicians? Or only kids who want to be world class chefs? No. *Their mission is simply to get kids off the street.*

If kids want to come in and goof off on video games, fine, they're off the street. They want to come in and learn how to cook? There are the tools to do that, too. And if they want to play basketball, great—here's a ball.

It may sound funny, but if more leaders in the world of network marketing would think like The Boys & Girls Club, their organizations would be unstoppable. They'd have so many people sticking around, that they would never want to leave that community. Ever.

When you get someone into network marketing, you're showing them a possibility of what life could look like, in other words, getting them *"off the streets"* in a way.

Now, some of you reading this are cringing at this idea. Maybe you're thinking I've lost it and I'm nuts, right?

Well, I'm not.

You know what the biggest benefits of being involved in network marketing are? Community, leadership, training, culture, and core values. Those are the *most* valuable benefits of network marketing—the benefits very few people talk about.

Okay Ray, but what does this have to do with being a freakishly effective leader? Everything! Network marketing is not only the product, service, and the compensation plan. It's all those things plus the relationships and friendships and community and culture and feeling good and awesome events and recognition and acknowledgement.

Do you truly want to become a freakishly effective leader? Then you might want to think about a mission that's bigger than just the money.

"Community" Versus "Transaction" Mindset

Ultimately, if your focus is solely on transactions (meaning the amount/number of sales and/or quantity of people recruited onto the team), you'll never become the leader you *could* be. Because a focus on transactions means you are only concerning yourself with obtaining more customers and more recruits.

I know what you're thinking: Aren't those things the point of the business? Ultimately, yes. And someone with a *transaction mindset* will make money, but they'll never make the *big money*.

Why?

Because people aren't loyal to a product.

In my first network marketing company I watched a guy go from nine years of paralyzing neck stiffness to being able to move freely after using our product. He was overjoyed with the results. Back then, I sucked at creating culture and pushed everyone hard to meet my level of desire and he was one that I pushed too hard. Two months later, he quit the business. The transaction of buying the product didn't create loyalty. In fact, I could make the case that once he solved his problem, he *transacted himself* off the team.

Always remember: People aren't loyal to products, they're loyal to a community of friends and family. Community is what wins. Ultimately, community defeats everything else.

What Makes for "Positive Culture"

Culture isn't just a group of people. How people are made to feel is part of the culture. Think of it like this: The sermon at a church is a part of the culture. The bake-off is a part of the culture. The carwash fundraiser is a part of the culture. The baptisms are a part of the culture.

So what is a positive culture in the world of network marketing? It's an environment in which everyone on the team feels good and included, regardless of their level of desire or level of achievement.

Look at why someone leaves any type of organization, it's almost always because there is a change in the culture, and the person no longer feels good being a part of it.

The best team cultures are the ones that aren't all business. Constant communication about money, scripts, prospecting and follow up will whittle away at your team. How to rank advance, make $100,000, and on and on and on—it simply wears people down.

No, to be a freakishly effective leader, you want to make sure there are lighter forms of communication, too. People don't just want to make money and achieve success, they also want to feel like they're having fun. Even better, they should *be* having fun.

The corporate world gets this.

Training for Culture

When you hear about a behavior that is against your core values or going against your culture, train on that. What do I mean? "Core values" refer to the principles of how people should behave in various situations. We will cover more on core values later.

We had a client with a big organization who had an issue that was causing a lot of drama. It was eating away at the culture she created. My suggestion was for her to do a training for her people on self-respect and respecting relationships, which was at the core of the problems she was having.

It worked.

You don't need to name names or call anyone out directly. That doesn't work and just raises resistance.

Simply talk about the behaviors you see that should be different. Talk about the core values. *Train on the culture.* By making it a training opportunity, you build up the culture and tackle problems in a constructive rather than destructive way.

Getting Engagement in Facebook Groups

One of the things I hear from networking marketing leaders is about their desire to create more engagement in their Facebook Groups.

Angel Fletcher, a good friend and a multi-year member of our TEC (Top Earner Club) mastermind group, is a top earner who had a total transformation with her group. We do hot seats with our TEC members and she saw one we did (called Lazarus) where I audited a client named Lazarus's team Facebook group. I basically tore it to shreds because every single post was about business, recruiting or money. Angel made changes in her group over the following few days and completely transformed the energy, engagement and even performance of that group. Angel says her group is now like Mr. Rogers neighborhood—it's fun, inspirational and full of love and encouragement.

Why is this so critical?

You need to understand the desires of the team. Remember, 80 percent of your team doesn't have a desire to become a big producer—they just want to be part of the group and have fun. And that's fine. You should love on them and appreciate them. Make them feel good to be a part of the team. If they're made to feel they don't belong because they're not striving hard enough to be super producers, they'll leave.

So, take some time and go into your group. Review the posts you've made and ask: Are they all about the money? Scripts? Recruiting or advancing in the comp plan? If they are, understand that about 80 percent of the group isn't being considered and most likely these individuals feel like they are disappointing you.

Make people happy they belong to the organization. Make it easy for them to stick around.

The question to ask is: How do we make this environment for people who are at different levels love being there so they don't want to leave? Make it a great place to be, and more people will catch the spark or at least stick around a lot longer, possibly on auto-ship (if your company offers that) and will feel happy about it.

Wisdom From Top Network Marketing Leader & TEC Member
ANGEL FLETCHER:

Great leadership is the combination of building, nurturing and loving on people where they are, all the while unlocking the potential they have. Great network marketing leaders inspire people to want to do things they normally wouldn't want to do so they can have more, do more, and become more.

The most common mistake I see leaders make is they try to manage people as if they were a "thing," and they forget that people are not possessions that can be managed. They are beautiful creatures that need to be inspired and influenced.

Struggles—or as I like to call them, "growing pains"—are never-ending in this profession because network marketing *is* based on eternal growth. With every next level there is a *next devil* that you must overcome. I truly believe that you grow yourself to the next level—and that in order to grow, you *must* struggle. The greatest obstacles one faces are self-created. Pride, ego and fear create far more obstacles than building a network.

The greatest benefit of being a network marketing leader is the person I have become in the process. I started out in this profession to change my family's lives. Then I decided to create change in the lives of others, and this is when the transformation happened in *myself.* Because my heart was aligned with serving my people, *who I am* completely changed. Today, I am filled with more love than I have ever known and I am living proof that you *give* in order to receive. Leading people has changed my existence on this planet.

Engagement From Other Leaders

Another thing leaders often ask: Shouldn't all my leaders be showing up in the group? Why aren't they in there, answering people's questions? They're not leading by example!

This might surprise you, but I think it's a mistake for you to pressure your leaders to engage more in the Facebook group. Different people have different personalities. If I were forced by my leader to answer 20 questions a day inside of the team group, I'd be unhappy. I'd rather be out prospecting, making money, doing other stuff.

It's fine. Don't push it.

On the other hand, there are people in your group—leaders and non-leaders, alike—who love engaging with others. *They love it!* They love loving on people and helping them.

Pick the right personalities to help you out with engagement. Don't dictate to your top producer: *"Hey, you need to get in there and congratulate people."* You don't want to take your top performers away from producing.

How We Created Engagement in Rank Makers

Not long after we launched our network marketing training group, *Rank Makers* (rankmakers.com), we realized we needed support. We needed to find people that really dug the group and would support and help it. We were also clear about the expectations. I went to the group and said, *"We're looking for people to help build culture within Rank Makers, and this is the criteria."*

Now, back then, we had maybe 2,000 people in the group. We told them we were seeking people who would be willing to invest at least five hours a week to help us out with this group. 78 people filled out the application! A whopping 78 said they were willing to give five hours a week, 20 hours a month, for no compensation. They understood we were on a mission and wanted to help as they believed in what we were doing. Today, the Rank Maker ambassadors are so important to us and the group. Although we don't compensate them financially, we reward them with special swag and extra love.

There are people with personalities who want to be involved, love on other people, celebrate and are willing to be your cheerleaders. Find them. They're out there. Utilize their talents. Often, they will NOT be your biggest producers "money wise" but good culture does not dictate that only producers can help with your group.

The Power of Personal Attention

As you bring people onboard, you can make them feel welcome. Your fast-start video can explain (if you need help with that and other leadership type resources you can check out HigdonGroup.com/teambuilder) that the team Facebook group is a resource for them. Also, from time to time when you can, send people a note that is just to them, not to everyone in the group.

For example, I take a lot of pictures. At last count, I had 10,691 photos on my phone. Seriously.

From time to time, maybe about once a month, I'll scroll through my photos, find an old picture with someone in it, and text, message or email it to them. And I'll attach a little note that says, *"Hey, just came across this photo, and it made me think of you. Hope you're doing well."* Not a group thing, but a thoughtful personal thing to do—a thoughtful, *personal thing*. Oh, and your company conventions are a great place to grab pictures with people on your team that you will be able to send out to them later.

It may not be a photo, of course. It might be something else. A voice message on a birthday. A card on their anniversary with the organization. A short email that says, *"Hey, I saw the advice you gave to Mary. It was perfect!"* Or if you see someone has a relative or loved one in the hospital, send a note and if you can afford it, flowers. Or if you see someone is struggling, either personally or professionally, send an email or voice mail that says, *"Hey, I'm here if you need to talk."*

Whatever.

The point is to start thinking about connecting with people in more personal ways.

At our company, The Higdon Group, we actually have a position called the *Growth and Gratitude Director*. That's all this person does. Their job is to send out gifts of appreciation; *to send out love*.

What can you do in your world? Whatever it is, it doesn't have to cost money. It doesn't have to be a gift. It can be something even more important. Like attention. And appreciation.

Discovering What Makes People Tick

So, how do you determine each person's level of desire? The first thing is always to start with the obvious, which is to ask. If they are a personal recruit of yours or someone on the team who comes into contact with you, ask them the questions mentioned below, however, don't assume everyone else you don't get to ask is a 5 percenter (see the Thompson Rule discussed earlier):

- *"What were the main reasons you joined?"*
- *"What do you hope to accomplish?"*
- *"How can I best serve you?"*

When you ask, don't take what they say as gospel. Many who told me they were going to crush it, never really intended to or had the desire. An unfortunate fact is 100 percent of the people who talked about all they were going to do for an extended time never did anything. So take your emotions out of it and love them for whatever they do even if it is directly against what they tell you they are going to do.

This is especially the case if you are a high-performing driver-type, because they'll want to gain your acceptance by telling you what they think you want to hear. Regardless, asking is always a good start.

Remember that a good culture makes people feel good regardless of their level of desire or level of results. It should not be only the producers who feel good in your group.

Leadership and Core Values

I talk a lot of about core values because they've always been important to me, and I believe they're important for any leader.

One of the definitions I saw online said that, *"core values are the fundamental beliefs of a person or organization."* It also said core values *"dictate behavior and can help people understand the difference between right and wrong."* Amen.

Core values are not only critical in network marketing, but everywhere—like, parenting. Good parents teach core values to their children, from a very early age.

There are two points I want to make about this:

- First, smart parents start teaching core values when their kids are still young and impressionable—when the lessons have a good chance of sticking, before bad habits are formed.

- Second, teaching core values and good habits to kids when they're young *(like brushing their teeth)* creates less work and less pain for everyone later.

None of this is to suggest you should treat the people on your team like children. But it's critical to recognize the importance of teaching people values as early as possible, especially when they are new and highly impressionable—before other bad habits or destructive beliefs have a chance to take hold.

Teaching core values to your team creates less work, not more as you are helping to alter the types of behavior that would create more work for you.

Be the Example, Not Just of Service

Many leaders pride themselves that they would do anything for their team. There is nothing wrong with that unless they are just being the role of a manager versus an active player. One of the best things you can do for your team is to be a great example by doing what you wish they were doing which is bringing more customers and reps into the organization. This flies in the face of the overtraining manager type leader. If your team is not moving, they most likely do NOT need more training from you.

Remember that anything you do, they think they also have to do. So the more you personally ramp up training and managing, they think they will have to do that as well at your rank and many of them do not want to do that. I know it sounds weird to hear from me, a trainer, that your team does not need more training, but I mean specifically from YOU.

When we train your teammates in Rank Makers, we always give them an action step and they realize I am not their upline and don't equate they have to do what I do or become me.

Being of "Too Much Service"

There are leaders who misunderstand the concept of serving others. They think it means *doing the work for others*. It does not.

One of the great leadership traps is when they end up doing *too much* for their downline. They spend enormous amounts of time and energy building people's teams *for* them, when what they should be doing is teaching people to utilize systems, resources and tools *to build their own team* and duplicate themselves.

Only Be Available for the Right Things

Often, new leaders act like a mother hen. If anyone comes to them with a problem or question, they will spend hours on the phone. Unless you are recording the conversation so it can go into a training archive for later, it's not duplicatable. For example, if you hop on the phone with anybody and spend any amount of time with that person, he or she will think that's what supporting people looks like. And they probably don't have that kind of time. So, in a way you're sabotaging them.

If anybody can get you on the phone any time of day for any reason, no matter what that person's activity level, you're not operating your business effectively. And this sets a bad precedent for others.

Celebrate Activity, Not Just Rank

When you only edify the people who have already made it, especially when you do it over and over, you miss opportunities to focus on the newer perhaps smaller successes that are happening.

I often hear of leaders who are doing some kind of recognition like *Diamond Tuesday,* and they'll recognize a Diamond that hit that rank six years ago, *but they haven't prospected anyone since then.*

Recognizing past achievement is a great gesture, but what does it really achieve? Nothing.

Look for the story that has happened in the last month, the story of someone who just got their first customer. The story of the person who just hit their first rank. The story of the person who has been struggling for a long time and finally did something. That's celebrating activity. *That's motivating.*

Fast success stories are typically more discouraging than encouraging. If you are going to share a fast success story, then be sure to add what that person has overcome in their life so people can root for them. Small or slow success stories are ones you should strive to share more often. Sharing that Lynda got her first two customers after being in the business for two years is very motivating to the majority of people in your team. Remember that the 5 percenters don't need much of this type of motivation, but everyone else does, and they make up 95 percent of your team.

The Truth About Duplication

There may be many paths to making money in network marketing, but the goal for the leader never changes—and that goal is duplication. That said, there is something you need to understand related to duplication that is wildly misunderstood in our profession. Here it is:

> ***How you attract people to you does not have to be duplicated.***

I encourage you to read the statement above again and again and again until you get it (which is why I asked my publishers to put the sentence in bold italics).

For example, it is now a well-established fact that it *is* possible to duplicate using social media. Yet there are many leaders who argue that social media is too technical and hard to learn—usually because they don't understand social media.

On the other hand, there are large numbers of leaders who believe that talking to strangers at gas stations and while in the checkout line is duplicatable, even though only a small percentage of any team will ever be willing to do that.

It's What Happens "After" That Matters Most

Whether people on your team want to prospect at a restaurant or car wash, or on Twitter, or at their son's karate class, doesn't matter. Sure, it may be important to *them*, but it shouldn't be important to you as a leader. Because how the contact was made isn't what you want to duplicate—it's what your team members do with those leads *afterward* that you should be concerned with—because *this* is where the magic of duplication takes place.

If the question of *how* people are attracted was the only way to duplicate, then you could never recruit anyone of authority. You could never recruit any doctors, judges or anyone who was chairman of a company, or anyone in politics, or a sports celebrity, or anyone with any kind of following or influence.

Because if you signed up a doctor, and that doctor placed the products in his waiting room—and that's how patients discovered the products and were introduced to the business—is that what would need to be duplicated?

No, of course not.

If that is what needed to be done to recruit people and duplicate, we'd all need to get medical degrees, open a doctor's office, and set up a waiting room complete with magazines.

It isn't *how* you attract people that needs to be duplicated. It's what you do *after* the attraction—what you do *after* the initial contact has been made. That's when the "system" kicks in.

Avoid Bashing People's Methods

Want to lose good teammates and cost yourself money? Bash ways of prospecting, recruiting or marketing other than what you do. I had people in my team that cold called, ran craigslist ads, and even had one guy that went from car dealership to car dealership to prospect. These are all ways I did NOT want to utilize!

But I never bashed those methods.

If anyone is attempting to grow their business, love on them. For instance, many trainers teach building rapport on social media, not realizing that most on their team don't know how to do this, how long it takes, or when to transition to business. As a result, many on their team simply don't do anything or send messages forever without ever asking if the person is open or not.

Often well-intentioned trainers or social media personalities will bash the "get to the point" approach that I teach because it's a tactic they do not use. This is an incredibly costly mistake as people who would have used that approach and gotten results will instead not take any action.

"There are many paths to making money in network marketing, but the goal for the leader never changes—and that goal is duplication."

-Ray Higdon

#FEL

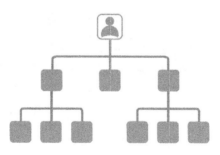

(Take a picture of this page and use #FEL)

Be the Role Model You Want People to Duplicate

As a leader, you need to make sure that you are coming across the way you want through your personal brand. Is it helpful? Is it educational? Is it uplifting? Is it attracting or is it self-centered and salesy? Everything you do reinforces it or erodes it. You get to choose.

Don't do anything you would NOT want your team to duplicate or attempt to duplicate.

I know many people classified as an MLM Leader that teach one thing but secretly do other things that are completely different...and they wonder why they don't have duplication.

Getting New People Started

If, as a leader, you think your new reps feel they need to do/learn everything before they talk to people, you're doing it wrong.

For example, say I joined your team and you told me, "Okay, Ray, step one is to watch all 57 videos in our company training library, they're really good." There's a good chance you'd lose me. I don't want to watch videos—at least not 57 of them!

The same thing would happen if you said, *"Okay, step one: Identify your target market. Step two: Create a powerful tagline. Step three: Think about how to launch your website."* And on and on and on. If this is your process for starting new reps, you're doing it wrong.

When new people feel like they've got to jump through a whole series of hoops and learn a whole bunch of stuff, you're not only *onboarding* them incorrectly, you may actually be headed toward *offboarding* them!

Onboarding People the Right Way

If you haven't taken the hint, you should never have a long, drawn out onboarding process. People don't need to know everything about the company, the benefits of every product, or minute details of the compensation plan before they move forward. The bigger, more complicated and more intense your onboarding process is, the less likely you're going to get the two things you really want:

1. *For the person to stay.*

2. *Duplication.*

There will always be the people who just have massive desire, grit and work ethic—so much so that even if your onboarding process sucks, they'll still make it happen. If your process is too long and complicated, you're going to blow off some people who would have made it happen if only you'd made things simpler.

Years ago, I would ask a new person: *"Who are the 10 friends and family members you are going to reach out to?"* And if they were reluctant to come up with the names, I would push them— and they would quit. So, I thought: *"How can I do this differently?"*

Then I started asking, *"All right, how do you want to build this thing?"* When I asked this question, people would always come back with the right answer. *Always.* How is that possible? It's because whatever they said, my response was, "Awesome. That's great!"

Now, in the back of my mind, I'm thinking about how I was going to get them to a company event and have them hear from other people about how important it is to reach out to their warm market. And when they did, they'd come away from the event and tell me, *"You know, Ray, I think I'm going to reach out to my warm market."* And I'd say, *"Awesome! Great idea."*

The best part of the idea was that it was *their* idea, not mine. They became the owner of the idea—*because it was theirs.*

Training in Logical "What If?" Order

Inside of *Rank Makers* (our membership group), we teach you and your people processes for prospecting, team building, and closing. And do you know what we teach first? *Closing.* This sounds a bit backwards, right?

Here's why closing is the first thing we teach:

If the first skill someone is taught is how to go out and find prospects, what happens when they're successful? What happens is the person reaches out to someone, and the prospect says, *"Sure, I'm willing to take a look."*

Okay, now what?

We call this asking the *"What if I get my wish?"* question.

What if they find a prospect, and the prospect is interested? They're not ready to proceed. They don't know what to do.

If someone gets a hot prospect, but they don't know what to do with them when/if the prospect shows interest, they're in trouble. They got what they wanted—a prospect—but have no idea what to do with them. Not only will this individual feel stressed, they will have probably burned a great prospect because they weren't ready and mishandled the situation.

It's like getting a fish on a hook but having never learned how to get the fish out of the water, off the hook, and into the cooler. The first thing we teach is the last step, not the first.

Who Are You Leading? (Four Types of People)

When CEO Jack Welch led General Electric, he identified four types of employees. While we don't have "employees" in network marketing, I share this because I think these four types are still accurate and helpful in leadership training.

- *Type One:* People who hit their goals and share the company core values. Leading this person is simple: You do it with love, appreciation, and keeping them around the team campfire.

- *Type Two:* People who *don't* hit their numbers and do *not* share company values. How do you lead this person? You don't. They need to go. In the world of network marketing, we don't fire people, but you don't have to give these people your time and attention. This may include that they need to be removed from your team group.

- *Type Three:* People who are not great performers, but they do share the company values. How do you lead this person? You mentor and help them get better. Someone who isn't performing at a high level but believes in your organization's core values is more important than a producer who doesn't.

And this brings us to the final type:

- *Type Four:* People who are producing, but don't share the company values. What do you do with this person? This is the toughest situation of all, but ultimately, they also must go. This is the toughest. Many leaders hang onto toxic producers for too long and lose a whole lot of would-be producers.

I once had a person in our organization who performed well when it came to delivering numbers but caused an enormous amount of strife and commotion among everyone else on the team. It was a serious problem.

Again, people like this can't be *fired*. You can't cancel their credit card and literally *boot them* from the team. But you don't have to give them the limelight, recognition or access to the group.

Some of you reading this are scared to do this. I understand. But not dealing with situations like this will keep your team from thriving. Other people see what's going on, and they know you're allowing the person to treat you and everyone else badly.

Cut off any producer who creates drama if you want to grow because one person's bad behavior can stifle 10 other potential leaders. Your good people *will* leave and go to another company rather than hang around in a negative environment.

Drama, negativity, cynicism, skepticism, and nastiness cannot be tolerated. If you lose a big producer, you may take a little dip. But in the long run it's so worth it because it separates out the real leaders who will have growing, lasting success. After all, Jack Welch wasn't a freakishly effective leader through weakness.

Great Leaders Make Things Easy

Remember the quote from Verne Harnish about leaders that I shared earlier? *"The role of the leader is to make things easy."*

I couldn't agree more.

Everything you suggest your team does needs to be put through the "Easier or Harder Test":

Is what I'm teaching people to do going to make it harder or easier for them? Harder or easier to be successful? Harder or easier to duplicate themselves?

If the answer is no, look for a simpler way. Keep it simple so anyone can do it regardless of background, credibility or even personality.

Some leaders have this big, 500-step technical mumbo jumbo process that includes having people set up their own website, shopping cart, merchant account—all kinds of stuff. The average person simply can't pull it off. And even if they *can*, they don't want to.

Complexity is the enemy of execution and will most certainly prevent you from hitting the big ranks. You need to ask yourself at every turn: *Can the average person, without a lot of time, without a lot of money—and without knowing about computers or social media—follow your process and succeed?*

If the answer is no, then you have a problem.

As such, I would never require people on my team to use social media. And if they did want to, I would instruct them in the most basic of ways, always making it simple and easy for them.

You never want to be there to "impress" people by sharing how smart you are with social media. Instead, make the business simple.

For example, I see way too many leaders on stage or in trainings assume their audience members have a certain (higher) level of education. They talk over their head for at least 90% of their presentation without even knowing they're doing it.

My goal was never to have people thinking how smart I am, but, rather, how simple the business is. So, I never hit people with 50 social media tips from stage, because people can't process that.

Now, that doesn't mean you can't share that stuff in a video—something that can be rewound, replayed, and transcribed for people to learn and study if they want. You may also want to do this in a blog. Doing this is effective and completely appropriate, if you're not introducing it too soon in the training and development process and making them believe they must know it *before* they prospect anyone.

Leaders Aren't Stingy With Giving Others Credit

My favorite boss from the corporate world, a lady named Maggie, told me once: *"If you want something done, be willing to give someone else credit."* Prior to that, I wanted all the credit for everything I did.

But she was right.

The goal for a leader should always be getting things done, not getting credit. Decide what you want to get done, enlist help from others, and then be willing to give away some credit. Better yet, be willing to give all of the credit—publicly to others—even if you were involved. Even if you were instrumental. Even if the thing was your idea, give the credit to someone else. Not only will you get things done, the person you gave the credit to will know it. And appreciate it. And then do the same thing, down the line.

Getting things done is the name of the game. Not getting credit. And don't worry, the bank will give you credit.

The Extroverted Versus Introverted Leader

People often ask: *If a leader is an introvert, is there anything different they need to do?* The bigger question is: *Can a person who is an <u>introvert</u> grow a team <u>at all</u>?* The answer I'm about to give might surprise you.

It is my firm belief that *introverts have an advantage over extroverts*—a major advantage, in fact. It's the *extroverts* that are at a *disadvantage*. This is the exact opposite of what most people think, of course. And the reason is: *The power of network marketing is in duplication, not in transactions.*

Here's what I mean.

In any other kind of sales, no matter what is being sold—cars, insurance, clothing, airplanes, whatever—the majority of people doing the selling are extroverts. And, as is the case for most extroverts, their success is often due to charisma, personality, public speaking skills, and other advanced abilities to persuade.

So, when an extrovert comes into network marketing, they do what they've always done—they use their extroverted skills and talents to recruit people onto their team. They call everyone they know and say, *"Hey man, I'm doing this thing. You know me, I'm going to crush this. We should rock it together, let's go!"*

When the prospect being recruited says *yes* and joins the team, the result is what we think of as a successful *transaction*—like when somebody buys a car or a computer, a *sale* has been made. But the extrovert has created a problem for themselves, because creating a *transaction* was only one of two goals. The other goal should have been creating a system of *duplication*.

The problem with using charisma and the power of personality as recruiting tools is that they can't be duplicated—*they're not transferable skills.*

When you approach people using personality and charisma as the primary tools for attraction, one of two things will happen:

1. *The person will sign up, thinking they'll need to be as charismatic as you are if they want to be successful, or...*

2. *The person will not sign up, because they think they'll never be able to duplicate your personality.*

This is why extroverts are at a disadvantage compared to introverts. Even if they get the person to join (a successful transaction) they've failed at the more important task, which is creating a system of duplication.

"The problem with using charisma and the 'power of personality' as recruiting tools is, they can't be duplicated—they're not transferable skills."

-Ray Higdon

#FEL

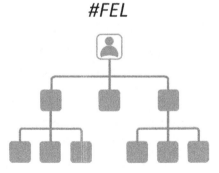

(Take a picture of this page and use #FEL)

The Introvert's Advantage

This is where introverts have an advantage over extroverts in network marketing. When an introvert recruits someone—using the tools created precisely for that purpose—they are demonstrating a system designed for duplication.

Now, when it comes time to teach people to prospect and recruit, the introvert is able to say, *"Just do what I did when I approached you. Use the tools and tell the company's story."* The result will be a sigh of relief. They'll say, *"Phew, you mean I don't have to learn big, long scripts? I don't have to be some big personality that I'm not? All I have to do is use the tools?"*

Yes.

That's all anyone has to do. Use the tools.

The tools are more powerful than personality because using the tools is a duplicatable process. As my good friend Eric Worre says, *"It's not about what works, it's about what duplicates."*

Extroverts often refuse to use the company tools because they feel they can do a better job with personality and charisma. And they're right, but only in terms of generating transactions—but not in terms of duplication.

The true power of network marketing is always in your power to duplicate yourself. And make no mistake: There are a lot more introverts out there than there are extroverts. So you better be thinking about training introverts to succeed, and that requires transferable tools of duplication.

If you are an introvert who has held yourself back from stepping into a leadership role because you don't think you have the "personality" to be successful, you are misguided. You can be just as effective, if not more so, as people who are extroverted and outgoing. If you are extroverted, it is essential that you rely on the tools that anyone else can use, stop focusing on your closing percentage, and focus more on bringing people in via a duplicable process.

Maximize Your Training Time

As mentioned earlier, network marketing leaders should never spend 45 minutes on the phone with someone, teaching them a skill or training them to do a task, without recording it. Here's why:

First, the person you just trained isn't going to remember half of what you said in 48 hours, and because you didn't record it, they can't ever play it back.

Second, when someone comes to me and says, *"Hey Ray, I want to reach out to a past co-worker. I'm just not sure what to say,"* I can say, *"Great question. There's a quick video over in the video archive that talks about that. Go check it out."*

Or if someone had an issue that I'd never heard before, and it's something that needs to be addressed, I'd say, *"I'll tell you what I'll do. I'm going to hang up and make a video on this, and we'll have it in the training archive. That way anytime you need to review it, or you have someone who needs to review it, just point them right there."*

This is maximizing your training time and serves as an example to your team. You're teaching them to maximize their time, and teaching people how to teach.

Reward Doing, Not Planning

When people are fired up about the idea of being a top earner, and are super motivated, great. And when they come to you and tell you they have a plan, provide encouragement. Being fired up and taking time to create a plan is a good sign. So, sure, they deserve a pat on the back. But simply having enthusiasm or even a plan shouldn't get them substantial time from you—*only their activity should.*

I did not understand this early in my career. I remember once recruiting a guy in Boston, and he said, *"Ray, listen man, I'm going to get a whole bunch of people to an event here, can you come up and present? I'll get 100 people in that room!"*

At the time, not understanding the difference between *plans* and *actions*, I hopped on a plane and flew to Boston. When I got there, the only person in the room was the rep himself. When he realized how bad he had overestimated what he could do, he made a few frantic calls and managed to drag his cynical, skeptical brother there. That was it. I wasted thousands of dollars flying up there. Worse still, I'd wasted my time.

If someone tells you they're ready to crush it and make it happen, that's great! But it doesn't mean they've earned your time.

Your Time Is Your Most Valuable Asset

When someone joins your team or buys your product, they don't own you. Being a part of your Facebook group or even getting your time and attention is not a right, it's a privilege.

You should be a lunatic about your time. If you give up your time too easily, you probably aren't being effective. You might think showing you care means giving all your time away.

It doesn't.

The other big issue is, you're teaching a bad paradigm. Your people see how easily you give up your time, and they think, *"Oh man, I couldn't be a leader. I can't give that amount of time away."* And they'll sabotage themselves because they don't want to become like you! By operating this way, you're causing yourself to lose money and people.

Leadership isn't just about developing skills and acquiring knowledge. It's about deploying your skill and knowledge effectively while operating in a way that doesn't turn others off. Don't get me wrong. Great work ethic matters. But if you do everything for everyone, you will sabotage people from working to get to your rank.

Assign Action-Based Homework

When someone joins your company, their starter kit doesn't come with a certificate of servitude from you. No one gets a ton of my personal time just because they're breathing oxygen. I get to choose whom I spend my personal time with. So do you.

When I was building a network marketing organization, how did I decide who got my personal time? Quite simply, I gave teammates action-based homework, sometimes with specific results-oriented goals attached. In other words, they had to earn it.

When a teammate requests your time, say something like: *"Awesome. The first thing you need to do is get out there and talk to 10 people. Then report back to me when you're done."* It doesn't have to be prospecting—though, from my experience, prospecting *is* a very effective form of homework—but you need to assign some kind of activity for the person to complete.

One day, a new rep on my team called and asked, *"What will it take to get you to come over to England and do a meeting with my people?"* I explained how I operate. I told him, *"Get 150 people on the team in your area, and I'll fly over there."*

He understood and said, *"Okay, cool."* About eight weeks later, he reached out to me and said, *"All right, I got it. Check my back office."* I checked his back office, and saw he'd completed the assignment.

A couple months later, I went to England—because he'd made it happen.

If people ask for your time, give them homework. *Specific, action-based homework.* Then, once they've done it, you can give them some of your time because they've earned it.

I am not saying to ever ignore your teammates. I am saying to be better with large amounts of your personal time. Too often, leaders invest an unlimited amount of time on someone who just wants attention, not results. You should care about your team, no doubt, but remember that you are also:

1) Teaching them how to treat you, and...

2) Being the model for them.

When People Aren't Getting Results

So, what happens when you assign homework, and team members come back to you and say: *"Hey, I'm doing everything you told me to do. I'm using the scripts you told me to use, every time, word-for-word, but I'm not getting results."*

What's the best way to handle it?

First, manage their expectations. Remind them it takes time to build a successful business, that results don't always happen immediately. (Note: These expectations should have been set long before this moment, preferably even before they come on board, so this is merely a healthy reminder.)

Second, trust that they're telling the truth, then verify to see if that's the case. And you know what? In the majority of cases when people claim they're doing exactly what they are told to do, but aren't getting results, they're really not doing it. They *claim* to be doing it. They *think* they're doing it. But they're not.

For example, I've had people swear up and down, *"Ray, I'm talking to people on social media the exact way you teach, I'm saying exactly what you say, and I've been doing this for 30 days and haven't recruited anybody."* So I tell them: *"Okay, send me some screenshots. Send me some screenshots of your conversations."*

(Note: I do NOT suggest you review everyone's conversations, do not become a crutch for them. But sometimes it makes sense for those who are doing the work to just do a check for them if they are frustrated.)

At this point, here's what usually happens: They don't send any screenshots, so maybe they weren't doing the work. Or they do send the work and they weren't doing what they said they were doing.

The truth is, there are people in network marketing who want attention more than results. This is important for any successful leader to understand.

"The truth is, there are people in network marketing who want attention more than results. This is important for any successful leader to understand."

-Ray Higdon

#FEL

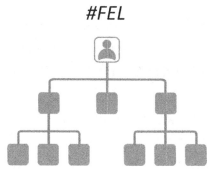

(Take a picture of this page and use #FEL)

Training Versus Inspiration

One mistake I see leaders make is they get so focused on the group that they stop producing themselves. Which reminds me of a story about the comedian Jerry Seinfeld.

There was this new comic who one night, before he went on stage, ran into Jerry Seinfeld. At the time, Jerry was already a legend in the business, and so the new comic asked, *"Jerry, what's one tip you can give me?"* Jerry responded, *"Commit to writing jokes every day. Get yourself a big calendar, and every day you do that, just put an x through that day, and create a daisy chain that never ends. I've been doing that for 29 years."*

No matter how successful he'd become, Jerry Seinfeld was still producing himself. Personally. Everyday.

Producing, for you, or for anyone in network marketing is asking people if they are open to your product, service or opportunity. Anything else is preparing for production but not production.

Leaders often fall in a trap, thinking the reason someone is not performing to their potential is because they haven't received enough training. Providing more training is usually not the answer. The problem isn't a lack of information. It is a lack of inspiration. Providing inspiration is the answer.

Making People Independent

Generally speaking, I have found that most people in network marketing look at leadership as *all the stuff they must do to run their team.* And they tend to think that if the role of the leader is done well, it is incredibly exhausting.

But leadership, if done the right way, is less work, not more. Again, think: easy.

When I was building a network marketing team, my goal was to turn people into warriors (the ones who wanted to become warriors, at least). I wanted to make them bulletproof, unstoppable and independent. Because to me, creating independent business owners—teaching them the skillsets they need, how to use the tools, and the core values for how they should show up in the world—that's *true* leadership.

The opposite of this is what I refer to as *nice* leadership. Nice is an acronym that stands for:

<u>N</u>othing <u>I</u>nside (Me) <u>C</u>ares <u>E</u>nough.

This is not to say that *nice* leaders don't do things for people, or that they're not being of service to others. To the contrary, *nice* leaders are of so much service that they adopt a *"let me do everything for you"* strategy:

- *Let me place the order for you...*
- *Let me do a three-way call for you...*
- *Let me... let me... let me...*

The *nice* leader hears their people trying to recruit someone on their own, and immediately says, *"Did you just try to recruit someone without involving me?"* And they're not saying it like, *"Yeah, way to go!"* That would be good leadership. They're saying it like, *"Why did you leave me out? You know I would have helped you."* And that's bad. Real bad.

You see, nice isn't nice. It's the opposite of being nice. It means:

- *Nothing Inside (Me) Cares Enough* to give you the tools you need to make it on your own.

- *Nothing Inside (Me) Cares Enough* to teach you how to make decisions without me.

- *Nothing Inside (Me) Cares Enough* to turn you into an adult, because I enjoy feeling like your parent.

- *Nothing Inside (Me) Cares Enough* to cut the umbilical cord to make you independent to run your own business without me.

The "nice" leader thinks they are doing good but, in reality, cripple their team from ever being independent while stunting their own growth as no one wants to be the mother hen like they are.

As a leader, ask yourself: What would happen to your beloved team if you were hit by a bus? If the answer is the team would crumble, then you aren't doing it right.

Making yourself indispensable is NOT the way network marketing is supposed to be. A major key in network marketing leadership, and this will be tough for some to swallow, is to make yourself irrelevant. The team should be able to produce without you and you should not have to be a slave to wiping their behinds.

Freakishly effective network marketing leaders are constantly asking themselves: *Are the members of the team equipped with the tools, the resources, the core values, the resiliency and the competency to move forward and thrive, build momentum, and change the world? Or, if I did get hit by a bus, would they be totally lost without me?*

Your goal as a leader is to make people *independent* of you, not *dependent on you.* Yes, you should be willing to roll up your sleeves and dig in to help people. But resist the temptation to make them reliant on you. Focus on creating team members who are so self-sufficient and independent of you they can proceed on their own—*and* feel great about it.

In the end, you—as the leader—aren't weighed down with tasks and responsibility. They're free, and so are you, which is why true leadership isn't really more work.

It's *less* work.

The Over-Teaching Trap

Leaders often believe the solution to virtually every problem is training. So they provide more training—and then even more training. Teaching your reps more and more is not necessarily the best idea.

Wait, Ray, isn't that all you do now? Teach? Yes, my company provides training to network marketing reps and leaders. The distinction is, that's *all* we do. But you, the leader of a team, have a lot of activities and tasks you could and should be doing other than teaching.

I'm a big fan of learning from your upline, but if the upline is doing a training every single day—I mean, like, going live and doing a training every single day—then, guess what? Some of the people will think that teaching every single day is something they have to do to reach your rank.

And that's a problem (two problems, actually).

- <u>One</u>: There will be people who either do not believe they have what it takes to train others, or they simply don't want to work that hard. They're going to say to themselves, "I don't want to be a trainer and that's what my upline always does. I don't want to do that."

- <u>Two</u>: If they *do* decide to replicate your actions, they become role models for over-training their people.

In either case, you may have sabotaged other people's success rather than help ensure it.

If you are in this over-training cycle, you may want to step back. Don't train just to train.

This is one of the reasons we've been so successful with our Rank Makers group—by providing a large portion of the training.

By the way, we don't ever do a training in Rank Makers without also providing an action step. This is a major reason why we average 60-100 rank advancements every single week.

This takes the load off the leaders while simultaneously showing the people on their teams how to utilize outside resources to get training done without necessarily having to do the training themselves.

The lesson here is an important one. Yes, people must get trained if you want them to be successful. But you don't have to do all the training yourself. Nor should you.

(For more information about what we provide at Rank Makers, visit: www.IsRankMakersLegit.com.)

When Someone Struggles

People often ask how long they should work with someone who just isn't doing what you've taught them to do. There are generally three reasons for this:

1. *They aren't willing to do the work.*

2. *They're apprehensive about taking action.*

3. *They're not in the business for results; they're in it for attention.*

The first situation is a matter of *laziness*, and people who are lazy want you to do their work for them. Don't fall for it.

The second situation is a matter of *fear*. Fear can be dealt with sometimes—not always, of course, because a person's fear may be so deeply rooted that it will never go away. But it's worth a try.

It's the third situation that is the most interesting and insidious. Because there are people who aren't interested in results at all—what they are seeking is your time and your attention. If they can get your time and attention, they're satisfied. They aren't playing for results. They're playing for attention.

The worst part of the situation? If you do give them your time and attention, you've rewarded them for not performing. You've given them what they wanted. Now, they'll want even more.

The best way to address any and all types is to find and share stories of small or slow successes in your company. Sharing that it took Joey two years to get his first customer and now is at a decent rank breathes hope into many people.

Don't Be Threatened by "Outside" Training

Leaders certainly don't have to invest in themselves and get outside training or coaching. However, one thing that costs them a lot of money and quality people is when they discover that one of their teammates has decided to invest in themselves with an outside trainer or training and they bash that action.

I have seen quite a few amazing people who loved their company and wanted to grow it, hire an outside coach or trainer and then get criticized by their upline. They hated the way that leader made them feel so much that they quit that company and joined a different team. Don't let this happen to you. There are people who don't want to promote outside trainers because they're worried their people will start following that person over themselves. Now, are there unethical trainers out there looking to steal your team? Unfortunately, yes. So, I would certainly be careful of whom you introduce to your team as there are some snakes out there. But to assume everyone is a snake is not a good idea, and it may cost you more money by losing good people.

You can't be paranoid that "everyone" is out to recruit your people. Likewise, you can't be afraid you'll get outshined by someone else while maintaining high quality people who are going to invest in themselves.

So, if your upline is telling you, *"Don't you dare buy training from anybody else,"* they're operating with a scarcity mindset.

In my case, I have always been a person who buys a lot of courses from a lot of different trainers. I invest in coaching, and I belong to a lot of masterminds.

When someone in your organization gets coaching or training from another trainer, say something like, *"Way to go! Awesome!"* Even if you don't like the person doing the training, you must react positively. Why? Because when someone searches for more information, it says the right thing about that person's tenacity and willingness to learn (independently, I might add). And reacting in a positive way says the right thing about you.

Get excited! The fact that they're searching for more information says they're serious about growth and want to get better at building a network marketing business.

Getting offended that people go around or outside of your leadership and teaching is a big mistake for two reasons:

1. *Your weakest people will stay (and probably talk about you behind your back).*

2. *Your stronger people will leave (regardless of how much money they're making).*

Never be threatened because someone gets training from someone else. Embrace it. And if you are threatened by it, ask yourself why. Is it because you know deep down that you need to grow and develop yourself to be a better teacher? A better leader? If the answer is yes, ask yourself which is more important: your ego or your income?

What Is a Personal Brand?

People are more confused about branding than probably any other topic in network marketing. This is largely due to the things they've learned from people who work in industries *outside* of network marketing.

Branding, in the way most people think about it, doesn't duplicate well. For many super well-branded network marketing "rock stars," the only shot they have at duplicating themselves would be if they brought in another rock star. That's a shame, because it shouldn't be only "rock stars" crushing it in your business.

Sadly, what we see is a lot of people who haven't even talked to or attempted to prospect anyone, and yet they are working on their tagline, figuring out their target market, and working on their big impressive brand. People could have opened their mouth to friends and family members—or even strangers—and could've already made money by now.

A "Brand" is Not a "Logo"

Yes, brands *do* have logos—Coke, Adidas, Ford, etc., all have logos—but their logos are not their brands. Logos are visual symbols, shorthand identifiers that stand for what the brand really is, which is...

A promise.

A promise of quality. A promise of reliability. A promise of creativity. A promise of excellence. A promise of change. More than anything else, it's a promise of how someone will *feel* and *benefit* by buying your product, using your service, or consuming your information.

Our company, *The Higdon Group*, has a brand strategy to provide high-quality information and strategies that improve people and their businesses. Every Facebook Live we do is part of our brand. Every blog and speech and article we write—*including this book*—are extensions of our brand.

What Is Your Personal Brand?

We all—through who we are, what we do, and what we believe—have already created a personal brand. Some people have established a brand of "hype" around themselves, while others have established a brand of being "pushy and demanding." Some have created a brand of being "workaholics," while others have branded themselves as "lazy."

And you? Do you have a brand?

Most people when asked this question will immediately answer, no. But of course they do. And so do you.

So what is your leadership brand? If I asked 20 people to give me three words that describe you, your brand would be obvious.

You Don't Have to Work on Brand-Building

First, understand that people don't *have* to develop a personal brand in network marketing. That should be obvious, because—long before our modern, high-tech times in which everyone seems to be branding themselves—people built large organizations. No branding, no blogging, no social media. Those things didn't exist. Yet people found ways to be successful in this business.

This is important because you may have people on your team who were attracted to your brand, and now they think they must have a big brand-based following like yours to be successful, too. This is not the case.

And you certainly don't want them thinking that is what being a leader is all about. That's why, when I was active in my business, I never went to my team and said, *"Hey, gang, you need to be blogging, you need to have a personal brand, you need to get professional photos."*

Building a Brand Requires Commitment

The reality is, it can be time consuming and costly to build a personal brand. As such, I warn people not to go down the branding rabbit hole unless—*unless*—it's something they really want to do.

I've known people in the business who went down the personal branding road, only to find themselves hiring their third web designer, their fifth graphics person, and crafting the fourteenth version of how to tell their story—and they were so busy doing all that, they still hadn't recruited anyone. I've also seen people become very, very successful, yet—if challenged—couldn't define what a brand was if their life depended on it.

Brand-Building Takes Time

If you're attracting people to your business by branding yourself, it's almost certain that people on your team will reach out to you, wanting to build *their* brand and attract people to them, just like they were attracted to you. And this is where you need to be cautious.

Before you start someone down the road to brand-building, it's important to ask questions about what that team member's goals are. If his or her answer(s) includes the word fast, you need to tell them the truth:

It's not going to happen fast.

It never does. *For anyone.* Building a personal brand takes time.

I always suggest that people go out and prospect, in person and on social media, and make it happen that way first. Get people making some money, and then if they want to venture down the branding path, you can help them do that. But the best thing to do is to get people to take small steps that lead to profitability, quickly. Get them to experience some success before giving them some huge, long-term marketing blueprint.

As discussed earlier, a person doesn't *have* to have a personal brand. Get them out there talking to people and using existing tools, company videos, etc. Your primary goal should be to get a lot of people in your team doing a little, not a few people on your team doing a lot.

Then go from there.

This doesn't mean I'm a fan of branding your company or product in your marketing. But if you're constantly posting your company name and/or product name on your pages or profiles then you are annoying many people connected to you and enabling anyone with interest to do their own independent research by searching the company or product name on google, amazon or eBay.

For extremely specific instructions on how to brand yourself in a way that duplicates, you may consider our Branding and Duplication Playbook at: www.HigdonGroup.com/playbook.

Wisdom From Top Network Marketing Leader & TEC Member
JEFF ALTGILBERS:

To me, being a great leader is always doing the right thing, even when it costs you and is hard to do. Keeping your word. It's never stealing a prospect or cross-sponsoring someone's leader. It also means to be available to your team and over-deliver what they need, when they need it.

The most common mistake I see leaders make has to do with ego—making the business about themselves, shifting their focus from *we* to *me*. They need to understand they can have anything they want if they have a servant-leader attitude. As leaders, we don't build other people's businesses; we just help them do it.

The other common mistake I see is around "expectation." Leaders expect too much from their team too soon. They try to manage and push, when what they need to understand is not everyone has the same goals. Get to know your key leaders better. Find out what they want and accept it. If you need leaders who perform at a higher level, keep hunting until you find them.

Network marketing leaders provide people the opportunity to achieve the most important thing any human being can ever offer another human: *time freedom.*

The freedom to be with their family. The freedom to travel with them to special places; to experience unique things together and build memories—memories they will cherish forever. To give to non-profit organizations. That's the power of great leadership.

Building Trust Through Transparency

Leadership gurus go around and tell people how important it is to *"be vulnerable."* What they really should be saying is: *"Be honest with people that you aren't perfect."*

In the corporate world, leaders create environments in which everybody comes to a meeting wearing a shield—a *mask*—something they hide behind so their boss and co-workers won't know their weaknesses and vulnerabilities. Because in *that* world, shortcomings aren't allowed and admitting them will hurt their chances for promotion.

But in the world of network marketing, it's the exact opposite—*especially when it comes to leadership.* When network marketing leaders admit to their shortcomings, everyone else around them starts to relax. People start to get that it's okay not to be perfect. It's okay to have weaknesses. It's okay not to have all the answers.

And in that moment, the freakishly effective leader—through their honesty—has created an environment in which others can stop or minimize beating themselves up for not being perfect. And this gives the leader the ability to identify real opportunities for personal development. This only happens when a leader creates an environment that makes those around them feel safe enough to say, *"Wow, I was struggling with something similar, maybe I'm not as bad as I thought."*

Transparency Rules!

The truth is, trust and transparency are not standard operating procedures on most teams, yet they should be. In fact, if you want to build a successful team that performs at peak levels over an extended period of time, trust and transparency *must* be present. I'll even go so far as to say that without trust and transparency, your team will eventually collapse under its own weight.

Sadly, what I see are leaders who act like they're working for a public relations agency, spinning everything that's happening to try and make things look like they're better than they are. Things aren't going well, and their response is: *"Everything's terrific! I've easily hit rank after rank after rank. I've never had any challenges or problems!"* They're afraid that telling the truth will weaken the team. Even more, they're afraid the truth will weaken their power over others.

The exact opposite is true.

You know what will forge your people (and future leaders) into steel? Reality. The nitty-gritty. The truth. The things people are often reluctant to share.

Sharing stuff that's real—including your fears and weaknesses— creates a bond, the importance of which is impossible to measure. And it prepares your team for the downturns they're bound to experience on the way to success, and you'll have a much stronger organization.

One example of keeping it real is sharing that, many times when you hit a new rank, you fall back the next month (or even for a few months after) and that it's common to not maintain a new rank.

Leaders who don't communicate this are really sabotaging their people. I have seen potentially amazing leaders leave a company because they were embarrassed that they couldn't maintain their new rank. They never knew it's quite normal to miss maintaining that new rank for a few months and that most leaders had a similar experience.

Building Better Culture

Some leaders think that building better culture in your group simply means doing more business trainings. Remember that culture is about making people to feel good regardless of their level of desire or level of result.

Instead of just doing business trainings, consider throwing pool parties or BBQ parties. One time we did a bubble soccer match (which was lots of fun). Think of ways that are cost effective and can be duplicated in other areas of the world to show your team you aren't just about business, but that you guys are a family.

Using Stories to Increase Event Attendance

When we were building our organization, we'd get hundreds of people on our team to the company event. How? We would look for success stories that came out of attending previous events, then go out of our way to share those stories with the team every chance we could.

An example of a story we would tell would be something like:

> *"Sally had been with the company for a year, without having much success. But within 30 days of attending the company convention, she's recruited her first five people!"*

The stories must be true and verifiable, of course—which is why they are so powerful.

Here's another example of a story we'd tell:

> *"I don't know what you'll get out of the event, but there was this guy named Dan, who was a construction worker, who went last year. He was pretty frustrated with his business, but when he came back from the event, he rank-advanced twice in 60 days."*

Typically, people promote events by saying things like, *"There's going to be great speakers, the lineup is amazing, the content is fantastic!"* And that's fine. But stories about people who attended previous events are more powerful than talking about who's going to speak from the stage at the next event.

They say that you make about $1,000 a year per person that you get to attend the company convention. I agree, this is a very good estimate. That said, how hard are you truly trying when it comes to getting people to your company convention? If you want to be freakishly effective, this should be a main focus.

Using Recognition Stories

One of the most impactful moments of my career was seeing a gentleman at a company event who was making $100,000 a year, cross the stage, and give his acceptance speech in sign language because he was born deaf. If you've ever had a tough conversation on the phone, well, he hasn't.

After that, whenever someone would tell me they couldn't do the business, I'd tell them the story about that guy. I'd say, *"Yeah, you're right. People have challenges. Speaking of challenges..."* and then I would share the story of this amazing man.

Rather than simply telling people they can do something, I tell them the story of someone who did—someone with greater challenges than they were facing. How do they argue with that?

The next time you're at your company convention, get your pad and pen out, especially during the recognition ceremonies when people's stories are shared. Because those stories are gold.

Don't limit yourself to using only stories from your life and/or your personal recruits. If there's someone in Saskatchewan who's not on your team but just achieved something great—or simply made their first $50 bucks—talk about them.

If the only story you tell is your own, people will think they need to wait to create stories of their own before using stories to prospect, train and motivate others. On top of this, being a great leader is about doing all you can to shine a light on everyone but yourself.

If you've got both arms wrapped around you, patting yourself on the back in both directions, there's no room for anyone else to talk about you. Tell stories about other people. Talk about others more than you talk about how impressive you are.

Side note: The worst thing you can do as a leader is skip the recognition ceremonies at your convention. Not only is doing so rude and unprofessional, you're setting a bad leadership example. The best example you can set is not only to attend and take notes, but also stand and cheer the people crossing the stage as loudly and enthusiastically as you can. When you're up there, being recognized, you'll be glad someone is there, returning the favor and doing the same for you.

Don't Overdue the Telling of "Big & Fast" Success Stories

As tempting as it is to think that sharing success stories is motivational to people, leaders eventually come to understand that the exact opposite can be true—especially when that success comes big and fast. For example:

Let's say Joe hits $10,000 his first week. That's awesome, and Joe deserves the love, no doubt. But there are a couple ways that you as an effective leader can choose to communicate this story. First, here's the wrong way: *"Hey guys! Congratulations to Joe. This guy came on board last week, and believe it or not, he's already made $10,000. Isn't that amazing?!"*

The majority of your team will be completely *turned off* by that. The goal was to motivate people and provide encouragement, but they will end up feeling discouraged, not encouraged. When you say stuff like this, it's a surefire way to get people thinking, *"I can't do that. What's wrong with me?"*

The Better Way to Motivate People

The better way to motivate people is to say, *"Hey, I have to share this. It's kind of a crazy story, but there's a guy that I met a few years ago, and he's been through a lot. He was injured in Desert Storm. He's been trying to build his own business for the last 27 years and just never could hit it big. And guys, all those different obstacles have actually helped prepare him. He came into this organization and hit his rank in his very first week! I know that sounds unbelievable, but let's give it up for Joe."*

Rather than moan, everyone will cheer.

More importantly, they'll cheer because they know the *whole story,* not just the success. They'll cheer the struggle.

So, when someone is crushing it, see if you can find out if there's more to the story. How long have they struggled? Did they go through a tough childhood or whatever? Did they lose it all at some point in their life? Try to find the downs, too, because if people learn the downs, they're usually very motivated by the ups rather than being jealous.

Also, be cautious not to overdo the *stage time* given to a single person, no matter how deserving.

I've seen people come into an organization, knock it out of the park, and suddenly they're on the company stage. They've accomplished what they were after, which was the limelight. Let them earn that. If someone new achieves fast success, give them love and attention—*but don't give them the keys to the kingdom.* They haven't been there that long. You don't know what's driving them. Because if what's driving them is the desire to be in the limelight, and you give them *too much* attention, they may go searching for a different limelight next month.

Somewhere else.

Focus on Your Story, Not Your "Stuff"

I never flashed a check or told people I was the number-one income earner in the company when I was prospecting. Instead, I focused on my story. I'd share how I'd lost everything in the real estate market, and how a buddy of mine invited me to a meeting. I'd tell them how I went with him, even though I wasn't sure what it was all about, and why I decided to join. I'd explain how my friend showed me what to do, and how I did the same thing—showing people how to make some extra money.

Flashing a big check or talking about your car is nowhere near as effective as telling your story. Your story—if you keep it basic and relatable—will draw people to you. Bragging about your income and showing off *your stuff* quite often does the exact opposite. It often pushes away good people.

Your Story Must Demonstrate Easy Duplication

There are some network marketing leaders who go out of their way to share how special, unique and credible they are. This is a mistake. If you are perceived as special, credible or unique, your duplication will suffer. You want everything you do to be an example of things the person you're talking to can do, too.

That's why showing off big checks is a negative for most people: It only leaves them thinking, *"Well, I don't have a big check to flash, how the heck can I do this?"* Freakishly effective leaders always get people thinking, *"Wow, I think I can do this!"*

This is the opposite of other types of sales. In other sales situations, being credible, unique, special and impressive is a positive. In network marketing, it's a negative.

Because in a typical sales situation, the salesperson has only one objective: Get the person to buy the product.

In network marketing, you always have two objectives:

1. *Get the person to buy what you're selling.*

2. *Show them that they can sell it, too.*

You want people to come away from every interaction believing they can do what they see you doing.

When you teach people to share their story, it should never be about how unique they are. It should always be about how normal and average they are, thereby resonating with the highest number of people to get them to believe they can also do it.

"Teammates should not get a ton of your personal time just because they're breathing oxygen. They have to earn it through their actions."

-Ray Higdon

#FEL

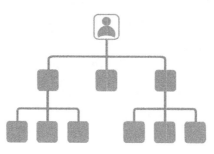

(Take a picture of this page and use #FEL)

Don't Oversell Your Work Ethic

Some leaders wear their work ethic like a badge of honor, bragging about how many meetings they do. Their need for attention has them trying to impress people with how long and hard they work. Their ego is running the show.

If they were being logical, they'd realize the person they're trying to recruit isn't impressed—they're horrified. *"Uh oh. I don't think I can do that. I don't think I can work as hard as they do."*

What's more, the goal should be to show people that network marketing is a way to decrease work, not increase it. Keeping it easy. Right?

When sharing your story and talking to people about your network marketing journey, try using this simple phrase:

All I did.

Instead of trying to impress people with how hard a worker you are, do the opposite and keep it simple.

- *"I couldn't even pronounce the name of the berry in our product! All I did was point people to the company video."*

- *"I didn't have a lot of time to put in when I first started. All I did was prospect in my spare time, a few hours each week instead of watching TV."*

- *"When I started, I didn't have anything even remotely close to selling skills. All I did was follow the system, and they either liked it and said yes, or they said no. It was that simple."*

Freakishly effective leadership is never about showing people how hard the business is or how awesome you are. It should be about how *average* you are, some of the things you have overcome, and how simple the business can be.

Be Relatable

The goal of any good leader should be to appear relatable at all times. Do you make videos with tons of trophies and pictures of you shaking hands with the president behind you? Hopefully not. When you introduce yourself do you include a bunch of credentials and throw around your rank? Not good.

For example, if you were coaching a doctor to recruit, you should teach her to say she works at the hospital—not that she's been a surgeon for the past 29 years. Working at the hospital is relatable—everyone's been to a hospital. Being a surgeon isn't. The last thing you want would be for others to think they had to be a surgeon to be successful and that's why they have success.

Our friend, Amy, has a great story about being relatable. She was in network marketing for 17 years and had made a grand total of $3,000 before becoming a million-dollar earner in her company. I told her to share the story about the $3,000, because $3,000 is so much more relatable than *"being a million-dollar earner."* Relatability and vulnerability are your secret weapons. They're more powerful than any bragging you could ever do because people relate with it.

On a personal note: Our business skyrocketed when I stopped trying to be big shot and started sharing my foreclosure story. Suddenly, everyone wanted to interview me on their podcast, have me speak on their stage. Also, more people on my team started believing they could create success. Interesting, huh?

Building "Expectation Resiliency"

Any leader who desires to achieve long-term success in network marketing must work at building what I call "expectation resiliency" within the team. This is done by actively communicating to your group that there will be ebbs and flows in the business.

Not only do you need to understand this yourself, you need to make sure everyone else understands it, as well.

Network marketing is not some magical world that is somehow unlike every other business on the planet. In the world of business, the market doesn't just go up, up, up, up, up, up, and never down. No business goes up forever without having some kind of dips in growth and/or financial performance.

Network marketing is no exception. It is subject to the same up and down market-forces and income fluctuations that all businesses are subjected to. Every company, including the giants—like Apple, Netflix, Facebook, etc.—experience periods of dramatic growth, followed by periods of performance recession.

This must be communicated to your people so that when the dips in performance appear, they don't freak out and jump ship.

Use Contests the Right Way

There are a few issues with contests leaders need to be aware of. The first is doing too many contests. The team's not doing much? I know! Let's have a contest! Don't get me wrong: contests can be very effective. But "over-contesting" can be a waste of time and effort. Too many contests can be a momentum-killer, which is the exact opposite of what you're trying to achieve.

The second issue is the almost-unavoidable flaw in the way most contests are designed. The flaw is having big rewards for just the top one or two recruiters because most people don't believe they can be the top recruiter. So they don't even try.

The Goal of Any Contest

The goal of any contest should be to provide incentives that motivate *everybody on the team* to step-up their game and improve their performance, not just your top people.

Our advice is to come up with something simple that most people believe they can do. For example, getting two sales. To get two sales, activity is required—and getting two sales is an accomplishment. Yes, it's not necessarily a big accomplishment but an accomplishment, nonetheless.

But what about the top performers? Two sales aren't going to get their juices going.

The best way to structure a contest that gets everyone involved is to say: *"For the top two-three recruiters, we're doing a dinner at the next event, and for everyone that gets at least two sales, you'll get an invite to a private training with Ray and be entered into a drawing to win a gift card"* (or a book, or whatever.)

You must have something that makes the top people strive to win, but also an incentive for those who know they won't hit the top one or two positions. The goal is to get a lot of people doing a little rather than driving more out of your top two-three people.

The Art of the Pre-Contest

The best way to start any contest is to have a pre-contest. It sounds like this:

> *"Hey, Everyone! In one week we're going to have a big contest with a lot of great prizes and fun things to win. If you'd like to participate in the contest, all you need to do is bring in one person in the next seven days and you'll be able to participate."*

Do this, and people who haven't brought in a soul in years will suddenly take action. They weren't even going to play in the big contest, but they believed they could bring in one. You'll have people show up that will shock you. Again, the key is getting people to do a little. Get more people to do a little more versus trying to squeeze more out of your big producers.

Someone will tell me they have three great producers and want to know how to get them to produce 10 percent more. Wrong thinking. Get a larger percentage of the entire team to do a little bit more.

Prizes and Duplication

Before you give a prize or incentive, remember that your people are watching everything you do. They are also asking themselves (consciously or subconsciously) if they can do what you are doing. This is why you want to be careful with incentives.

I've known leaders who make $30,000 a month, and they spend $20,000 on prizes and other incentives. That is not only unduplicatable, it's not smart. Not only are these leaders going to have trouble paying their tax bill, other leaders (and potential future leaders) in the organization see that and think, *"I could never do that."*

And they shouldn't.

Wisdom From Top Network Marketing Leader & TEC Member

NICOLA SMITH JACKSON:

A great network marketing leader is able to inspire and motivate others to action through results in a systematic way. They create an atmosphere that gives vision and builds belief where the ordinary person can begin to experience extraordinary results through passion and consistency.

If you are a leader, I encourage you to take ownership for your success by learning the principles and systems of the industry and your company. Build your business with simple systems that people can follow and duplicate consistently.

Leaders should create a culture where there is a daily method of operation, where the focus is on a core obtainable title that can easily duplicate. This creates momentum and turns ordinary people into super producers.

Never stop recruiting or looking for new talent.

A leader should not forget where they came from and remain humble through their success journey. The mission is to build belief that success is obtainable. This breeds encouragement in a team and is key for long-term success.

Make a habit of investing a dedicated portion of time and money into personal development to learn skills and strategies that encourage better communication, team production, collaboration and cooperation. This will make you stronger and wiser.

"Negative Up, Positive Down"

One of the most important communication concepts of effective leadership is contained in this simple, four-word rule:

"Negative up, positive down."

It means you should communicate negative information *up* the line, and positive information *down* the line. For example, let's say product shipments have been coming late and people on the team are complaining about it. Your responsibility is to communicate the negative situation to other leaders in case they're not aware of the situation. *Negative, up.* Then when you get feedback about how the problem is being addressed, you communicate the solution to your downline. *Positive, down.*

Freakishly effective leaders set an expectation that if someone has a problem, they don't go around creating drama, calling, texting or posting to the group. They need to communicate *up* to you. And when you have an issue, you never go downline with negativity.

What Brings Success to Most Leaders

What gets most leaders to a high rank, as I see it, are the following three things (in order of importance):

> *#1: Prospecting quality people for their team.*

> *#2: Constantly referring to the tools and system and getting people to events.*

> *#3: Getting training resources to their team (their own training, Rank Makers, script books, etc.)*

But just when many leaders achieve a high rank, they stop doing the very things that made them successful. They forget who and what got them there. They shift from actively *building* the team (and improving the skills of people on it) to trying to be "super trainer" or expecting all growth to come from their downline.

Big mistake.

Because once leaders stop doing the activities that brought them success, the level of success they've achieved typically begins to evaporate—slowly, at first, so the decline is barely noticeable. Then they start to notice.

Pay Attention to What Got You Here

Many leaders—once they achieve the desired rank or position in their organization—get hung up on their status. They forget what got them there.

Notice I said **what** got them there, and not **who** got them there.

The team that got you to your current status may not be the team that gets you to the next level. This does not mean to ignore or mistreat who got you to your current rank. But remember what activity it was that got you where you are and keep bringing new people into your organization.

In my opinion, *this* is the biggest mistake MLM leaders make. Once they reach a high rank, they forget what got them there. They stop doing what made them successful and got them there in the first place. Not only have I witnessed this numerous times over the years, but others have told me they've seen it again and again, as well.

Maintaining Rank

Earlier I talked about "expectation resiliency," and this is a part of that, and also something you may not want to hear. Many people don't talk about this or teach it, but it's important to let people know that when they reach a new and/or high rank, the chances of them maintaining that rank the next month (and perhaps the month after that) is extremely unlikely.

Ouch.

If people aren't taught this and it happens, it will come as a major shock. They hit a big rank and they're super excited and fired up. They're proud, of course, so they tell everybody.

Then the next month, suddenly they don't make it. Now they're embarrassed and don't want anybody to know. Their internal dialog starts going, *"Oh, no, I didn't hit it this month. Oh my God, I don't want anyone to find out!"* They feel like a fake and a failure (even though they're not, since this is a very common turn of events).

Had they been taught this was a common thing, all this internal angst could have been avoided. Also, they'd then know to teach the same thing to their people going forward.

Maybe this has happened to you. If so, don't freak out—just get back to doing the things that got you there in the first place.

Being "Outranked" As a Leader

In my experience, the majority of big earners outrank the person who sponsored them. So, what if someone you recruit onto your team eventually outranks you?

First, if you're reading this right now, it means you are motivated to grow your business, so it shouldn't be easy to pass you up. However, even if you're driven and doing the work, it can still happen. And if it does, that's awesome. Why? Because...

The only thing better than being a diamond is being a diamond-maker.

For me, I wanted people to pass me up (which is not to say I was going to make it easy). And you should want as many people in your organization to do as well as humanly possible.

I find that people who reach leadership status generally fall into one of two categories in the world of network marketing:

1. *People who are in it to earn big money and make a big impact.*

2. *People who are in it to stroke their ego.*

If you are currently someone who is bothered because someone passes you up, your ego is costing you money.

People who are in this profession to stroke their own ego are bothered by the idea of someone passing them up, even though they'd be earning a cut of that person's production forever.

If you want to make big money, you need to learn to leave your ego at the door. If you want to make small money, fine—focus on your ego.

Disappointment in the Team

What do new leaders do if they start to build a team and then suddenly people start to drift, and they start losing people? How do they deal with the disappointment? Do they just continue the way they have? Or should they stop and analyze the situation?

Let's start with this:

When you bring people onto your team, regardless of what they tell you (or what you may know about their past performance in another company), half of you should believe they will become the greatest performer you've ever had, and the other half of you should assume they'll be quitting tomorrow.

Here's why:

- *If they apply themselves and work at growing their business, you'll be prepared to support them, but...*

- *If they decide to leave tomorrow, you won't suffer any disappointment from the loss.*

The important thing to understand is that your emotional reaction to either event, on either end of the spectrum—success or disappointment—is *predetermined* by the expectations *you* create in your mind from the outset of the process.

If you totally buy-in to someone's declarations about how hard they're going to work, and how big they're going to grow their business—*("This person is going to be a total game changer for my entire business!")*—you set yourself up to be blindsided if they don't perform at that level. On the other hand, if you assume a person will leave—*("I'm not lifting a finger to help this person no matter what, because I know they're eventually going to leave!")*—you may end up neglecting the person, which contributes to them doing exactly that.

The only rational approach is to take both positions, at the same time: *The person may stay and work their rear off, so I need to be ready to support them if they do, <u>and</u> they may decide to leave, so I shouldn't be too surprised, either.*

When People Leave for a Different Company

One of the questions I get a lot is: *What should I do when people leave my team for a different company?*

First, you need to understand that you can't stop it. It's going to happen. No matter how charismatic you are, no matter how great your culture is, there will be people who leave—especially in this age of social media.

Years ago, we weren't connected globally like we are today. People didn't know what they didn't know; they simply didn't have access. Today, everyone has access to everything! Which provides people with virtually limitless options.

- No one has 100 percent retention.

- No one retains all their people, and they lose some of their key leaders, too.

And if you have yet to have a leader leave your team, be prepared—it *will* happen.

"Leaders in network marketing who have an ego problem will be more focused on controlling you than helping you see results. Doing anything outside of their control will reveal their true colors."

-Ray Higdon

#FEL

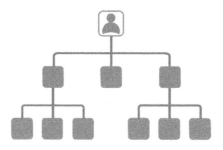

(Take a picture of this page and use #FEL)

What Can You Do?

Okay, so people will leave. But this is not to say there's *nothing* you can do, that you should just stand back and accept it without a fight.

Here are four things that will help you handle this situation:

1) Focus on Breaking Your P.R.

If you've ever run track or cross country, you're familiar with the term P.R., which stands for *personal record*. In the world of network marketing, we have personal records, too: a record for the amount of product we've personally sold, a record for the total dollar volume of our team/downline, and—of course—a record for the number of people we've recruited to join our team in a week (or month).

When I would have someone influential in my organization leave, I would set a goal to go out and break my personal record for the number of people I'd recruited onto my team in a 30-day period, with a new P.R.R. *(Personal Recruiting Record)*. I would decide it wasn't time to curl up in fetal position and cry, but, rather, a time to step it up.

Why did I do this? The obvious and somewhat surface-level answer was to replace the person or people who had left. But that's not the main reason. The main reason is because I knew that, when people heard about the person leaving, they were going to watch to see how I was reacting. Is he angry? Is he slowing down because he's depressed? Is he going to start bashing this person?

When someone would leave my team, I went out of my way to make sure people saw none of this! Instead, I wanted them to see me focusing on going forward, not back, by bringing in new blood—people who were fresh and excited about building the business.

This is critical because people will be wondering about you. Are you going to leave, too? When another leader leaves they will be filled with a sudden sense of fear. And doubt. As a result, they might slow down, stop prospecting. They'll wait to see what you're going to do. And when they see you bringing in new people, you will erase their concerns.

2) Analyze Your Garden.

In the company where I was the number-one income earner, I had my number-one leader leave, and I didn't skip a beat. My income didn't go down. Yes, there were some people who jumped with that person, but none of them were the people I really wanted to stay. The leaders underneath that person—the ones I really hoped wouldn't leave—*they all stayed.*

The main reason they stayed was because I'd gone out of my way to build relationships with them.

Analyze your garden means asking yourself: *Are you connecting with enough of your leaders in your organization?* Look at your team culture and ask:

- *Is your culture one of acknowledgement and making people feel good regardless of their level of desire or level of result?*

- *Do you spend time on acknowledgement and recognition, or is it all about you?*

- *If it's all about you, and you took that leader who left for granted, then ask yourself, how can you get better? What can you learn, how can you improve? What can you make better? Did you not show them enough love? Did you not connect with them enough?*

When I would recruit someone who had a history of jumping, I understood there was a good chance that person wouldn't stay. Knowing that, I made it a point to connect with the people they brought into the business. If it was clear that someone had the potential to become a rock star, I would send that person a thank you card or a gift. I'd message them, *"Hey, way to go. I hear you're crushing it. Awesome!"* I always went out of my way to establish a relationship with them.

3) Don't Bash People or Other Companies. Ever.

Don't, don't, don't, don't, don't, don't, don't, don't, don't, don't, don't, don't, don't, don't—never ever, never ever, never ever, ever, ever, ever, ever bash someone who has left your team. In fact, let's just expand that to be *anyone*, period.

Ever.

I cannot stress this strongly enough.

Before I entered network marketing, I worked in real estate. I decided to stop being a speaker for the real estate organization I had been working with, and I'd gone out of my way to leave on a good note. Yet, over the next two years, they bashed me anyway.

That organization actually sent out an email to their entire list about something I was offering on my website, telling everyone why what I was offering was a bad deal. This email—*designed to bash me and what I was offering*—went out to tens of thousands of people. They even included a link to *my* website in *their* email! Unbelievable, right?

Here's what's interesting:

As a result of their email, I had more traffic on my website than I'd ever had: *traffic that helped me sell the deal I was offering.* The funniest part is, until that moment, the offer wasn't selling. It was only *after* they bashed me that it started to sell.

Bashing others often leads to unintended consequences, like playing Russian roulette. For example, if I say, *"Hey everyone, don't talk to Tracey because she's left us. Tracey is bad."* Well, guess what? Anybody who knows Tracey and likes her even a smidgen will go out of their way to find out what happened. They may even call her to find out. It will not just result in an unintended consequence but the exact opposite of what you wanted.

The only things you should ever bash are unwanted behaviors. For example, sometimes people will try to lure others away by saying things like, *"Our comp plan is better."* The truth is, it may pay more on the front end, but the residual is terrible. If something like that happens, don't name the company. But do talk about how in your history of network marketing, you had been told by companies that they had *"better comp plans"* only to realize you had to recruit a ton more people every single month to make the same residual you're making in your current company.

Bash the behavior. Bash the shiny object that others are dangling to lure your people away. But never name the person, or the company.

4) Be Big, Wish People Well.

Now, this may be challenging but it's important.

I had a major leader leave my team once, and he immediately started saying negative things to people about me. I had done nothing but support him while we'd worked together, but he still bashed me. It was frustrating and confusing.

The only thing I could figure was that he assumed I was going to attack him for leaving, which was probably what he'd experienced in the past. So he was beating me to the punch.

As disappointed as I was with his behavior, I decided to take a different tack. Rather than bash him in return, I reached out to him, telling him how sad I was to see him go. Which was true. I also told him I'd heard that he'd said some negative things about me but good luck—and that I hoped the company he was going to worked out for him (which was also true, because I wished him no ill will). Then I told him that if I could ever be of help, he should feel free to call and let me know.

And I meant it.

A few years later, he actually reached out to me—and hired me as a coach.

When you lose someone, even if the person bashes you and hurts your feelings—even when it hurts—be the bigger person and wish them well. There is always a chance that they'll come back. And if you're nice, chances are good they'll stop with the insults.

If someone does leave, just work on being better. And don't get consumed with the notion that certain people must stay in your organization forever, no matter how much you've done for them. Too many people dwell on that. And it's a waste of time. Get over it. Move on. That's part of what being a freakishly effective leader is all about.

"Single-Person Issue" Versus "Team Issue"

A big flaw of leadership is taking a single incident, or a small handful of incidents, and applying them to everyone. For example, I've had leaders over the years say, *"Oh man, all of my team is leaving."* So, I'll ask, *"Okay, tell me who?"* And then it turns out that everyone leaving was actually only two-three people. Freakishly effective leaders need to avoid absolute thinking. Nothing is ever absolute.

- *"Everyone is leaving."* Really? Everyone?

- *"No one is doing anything."* No one? Not a single one?

- *"Nothing is getting done."* Really? Nothing?

- *"My entire team dislikes me."* Really? The entire team? Every single person on it?

I've had leaders over the years tell me, *"My team isn't doing anything."* Upon inspection, it turned out *lots* of people were doing something. Making blanket statements debilitates you as a leader. And God forbid your team ever hears you say things like that!

How do you think the people who *are* working will react when they hear a leader say something like that? Blanket statements are without a doubt the fastest way to sabotage your team and bring people down.

When leaders say ridiculous, inaccurate things to their teams, the impact can be devastating. So be accurate in your analysis of any situation. Because your interpretation of what you believe is the truth impacts your next action. When your assumptions about people and results are wrong, your future actions will be ineffective and produce failure.

When to Boot Someone Out of Your Group

So, what do you do when someone is behaving inappropriately, being sarcastic, cynical, negative, and causing drama for the team?

First, understand that some people are just oblivious to what they're doing and saying; they just don't realize the impact they're having. They just don't get it—they're naïve. In such cases, I have found that simply calling their attention to the situation solves the issue immediately.

There will be other situations, however, where the problem isn't the result of a lack of awareness or naiveté. The negative behavior is intentional, maybe even malicious. When this is the case, you'll have to go a bit deeper when you address it.

In either case, it's important to be nice and respectful to the person you are dealing with. This person's lack of good manners is never an excuse for you to behave similarly. Also, in your communications, be specific. For example, if someone is being overly negative in the group, don't just say, *"Hey, you're being negative, knock it off."*

Get a screenshot of one of their negative posts and send it to them. Then explain it:

> *"Here's a screenshot where you made this comment. This is negative, and we want to prevent this kind of stuff from injuring the group. I'm sure you don't mean to stir the pot or create negativity, but I'm giving you a heads up that we just can't have that kind of stuff in there. If I have to address it again, you can certainly still be a part of the team, just not part of the group."*

Also, whatever you do, never warn someone and then fail to follow through. That is just as bad, maybe worse, than letting bad behavior continue unchallenged.

I have found, from my experience, that if you don't address situations directly, the person isn't going to get it. Worse still, they may know exactly what they're doing, and they don't care and/or enjoy being disruptive. And when you don't address it, they'll start to question your leadership, and things will only go downhill from there.

Avoid "Celebratory Finality"

First, in case you don't know this about me, sometimes I like to make up my own phrases. *Celebratory finality* is one of them.

Celebratory finality means accomplishing something so completely, it's literally the best you can do—to the point of actually celebrating it.

For example, we have a TEC client named Mary who has hit the top rank in the European market. And that's what she'd tell people: *"Hey, we've hit the top rank in the European market."* I know what you're thinking: *What the heck is wrong with that, Ray?*

The problem is that words are important—especially if you speak them to others. In this case, when Mary told people she'd *"arrived,"* she was unintentionally setting herself up for slowed growth. Why? Because, as the dictionary defines it, to *arrive* is to *"reach a place at the end of a journey."* The *end* of a journey.

Again, you're probably thinking, *"Jeez, Ray, we're really getting down in the weeds here."* Yes, we are. And trust me when I tell you, if you're going to become a freakishly effective leader, you're going to find yourself navigating the nuances of leadership and getting into the weeds a lot because everything matters. *Everything.*

Especially your words.

So, I coached Mary to stop saying, *"I hit the top rank in the company"* and instead say *"I hit the current top rank in my company."*

There's a subtle but important difference between the two statements:

- The first says arrived at the end of the journey. *The second says the top rank for now.*

- The first marks the end of the road. *The second says there's more road ahead.*

- The first is limited. *The second is empowering.*

- The first has *celebratory finality* to it. *The second suggests progression toward the next milestone.*

And just in case you don't think stuff like this works, we've had clients who'd reached the "top rank" but continued crushing it so hard the company actually created a new *higher* rank. I don't think that would have ever happened if they had operated in a psychological world of celebratory finality.

Final Thoughts...

Many people think that motivation is the ability to get people to do things they're unable to do. It's not.

Motivation, from a leadership perspective, is about getting people to do things they're fully capable of doing *but won't do without being reminded why they should do them*. Like, for example, prospecting and recruiting.

There's no such thing as someone who is incapable of prospecting and recruiting. These are perfectly learnable skills, by anyone. *Anyone* can prospect and recruit if they want to, which is part of what makes network marketing so powerful.

The key words in the previous sentence, of course: *want to*. Because the key to success isn't the ability to do the work—*it's remembering why you started and why it's important to keep at it*.

This is where freakishly effective leaders earn their keep, by creating a vision of what the future could look like, then taking the time to remind them of that vision.

Nine out of 10 times, when someone fails to do the things that are necessary for success, it has nothing to do with ability. It's not that they *can't*—it's that they have lost their focus and forgotten why they got into the business in the first place.

The Importance of Leadership "Vision"

When you think about vision in network marketing, it starts with the company founders. That said, as an individual leader, your vision matters greatly—you also need to have a vision.

A freakishly effective leader makes people feel like they're part of something bigger than themselves. They paint a picture of what's possible, for each person on the team as individuals, and for the team as a whole. Painting this vision, and communicating it regularly and well, is an activity worthy of your time. And it feels good.

Our Mission is to Make Your Job Easier

I hope this book has helped you with some of the issues you have experienced that perhaps have slowed you down. Having worked with many companies and many leaders, we are constantly innovating methods to make your job as a leader easier.

You might consider getting a copy of this book in the hands of your other leaders and inviting your team into our Rank Makers group where I kick their butts on a daily basis.

We believe having your teammates read this book and get involved in our group will make your job (and life) easier.

Either way, we want to thank you for choosing to be in what we consider the greatest profession in the world which is network marketing. And we believe network marketing is the lowest risk, lowest overhead way for the average, ordinary person to start and build a business.

We are honored to work with leaders and companies that make a larger impact and are grateful you've allowed us to help you on your journey.

#1 Amazon Bestsellers by Ray Higdon, available in Kindle, paperback and audio at Amazon.com

About the Author...

Ray Higdon is a two-time best-selling author and a former number-one income earner in a network marketing company he joined while he was in foreclosure. He has shared the stage with Tony Robbins, Bob Proctor, Les Brown, Robert Kiyosaki and many more. Ray and his wife no longer build a network marketing company so they can better serve the profession as coaches, speakers, and trainers. Ray blogs almost daily on www.RayHigdon.com and is the co-owner of the Higdon Group.

Together, with his wife and business partner, Jessica, The Higdon Group, was recognized on the Inc. 5,000 as one of America's fastest growing companies. More than anything else, they love helping network marketers grow large teams and create freedom in their life.

About Rank Makers...

Rank Makers is a worldwide community dedicated to becoming the highest producing group inside the network marketing profession. Rank Makers is our private group where Ray goes live every single day with a training and action step for your team. Since  its inception in July of 2017, we have helped create well over 4,000 rank advancements in all different companies and countries. If you have people that simply don't know what to do each day to grow their business, let us help you create momentum in your group. Feel free to visit or share with your team: RankMakers.com.

Are You Ready to Shortcut Your Way to Grow a

MASSIVE TEAM

with Your Network Marketing Business?

Get Your Blueprint Now At:
teambuilderblueprint.com

I want to PERSONALLY show you how it's possible to accelerate your team growth without spending more time or working harder. **Learn 21 ways to boost your team building, leadership, & duplication** *(so you can make more money faster, easier, and in much less time!)*

Comes with Two Free Bonuses!

BONUS #1: How to Create a Presentation for Your Network Marketing Company *(so you and your team have a powerful marketing TOOL to point new prospects to saving time and allowing you to talk to more people)* - **$325 Value**

BONUS #2: Creating a Network Marketing Fast Start Training *(so that you invest more time prospecting & recruiting while training new reps on how to get into action building their team)* - **$598 Value**

Get Your Blueprint Now At:
teambuilderblueprint.com

Want Us to Blow Your Audience's Mind?

For information about having Ray and/or Jessica speak at your next event, email our team at:
support@RayHigdon.com

Made in the USA
Las Vegas, NV
28 August 2022

54213344R00066